Your Time Is Now

by Serena Carcasole

Dedication

This book is dedicated to my Dad. He is no longer with us, but will always live in our hearts as the best Dad anyone could ever ask for.

To my husband and daughter, for being supportive throughout my journey and desire to live the life of our dreams while helping women globally do the same.

To all the amazing women in my network who have the same mission and passion to make an impact.

And last but not least, to my incredible team for helping turn my wishes into reality.

Contents

Introduction

Dear Reader,

I'm so glad you're here, because it's time … time you knew that you have within you everything you need to control your destiny!

My mission, captured in these pages, is to help you—and women all over the world—to go for your dreams.

In reading these stories, I hope you'll be inspired to transform your mindset and take action that aligns with your biggest dreams … because you CAN make them a reality.

The day my father died, I made a promise to myself to cultivate an abundance mindset, so I could live for today.

That mindset is what gave me the strength, a few months later, to walk away from my corporate job and start my own business.

And that completely changed my life!

Now, I hope this book will help change yours.

This book is a collection of stories by and about a variety of women who are as unique as they are vibrant … as inspiring as they are brave.

One thing they all have in common is that they took the leap: they realized that they could take action to create and live their dream lives—and they did.

Every woman who contributed to this book wants you to know that there is no failure if you believe you can go for your dreams, and take action to do so.

We want to help you have the life of your dreams, too.

That's why each contributor shares a complimentary gift designed to guide you in taking action to create positive change in your life, starting now.

There is no failure when you access and use the resources available.

There is no failure when you're inspired, educated, and empowered.

And, as you read through the stories in this book, I know you will be.

You can start living your dream life, today, built around a business that utilizes your gifts and passions.

Your time is now!

Chapter 1

Stop Waiting, Start Living:
Why NOW Is the Perfect Time to Pursue Your Dreams

By Serena Carcasole

"It's inoperable," said the oncologist. "I am so sorry. Your dad has nine months to live."

It was the worst day of my life.

This can't be happening, I thought. *He's only 56 years old.*

Heartbroken, and in a state of utter shock, I felt the weight of hundreds of bricks fall on my shoulders.

How can this be?? He is too young! Why him? Why me? I don't want to go through this pain. We need him. He is the glue that keeps our family together. How will this affect my daughter? She's only three, and they're so close. How will it affect my little sister, at 19?

In 2007, my father passed away ... and it changed my entire life.

On one hand, I began to experience what would become chronic health conditions as a result of stress.

On the other hand, the timing of his passing taught me an important lesson ... one that helped me liberate myself from a job and lifestyle that didn't serve me—and set me on the path to help others do the same.

I was working for a corporate company, and my managers didn't support me when I needed to take time to deal with family matters and emotional bereavement. I went on stress leave, which seemed like a negative ... but it ended up being a wonderful new path on my life's journey, because it gave me the opportunity to start my own business.

For years, my dad had dreamed of buying a big truck (SUV) as soon as he finished paying of his mortgage. He didn't want two big payments; he thought it was too much to handle, that it would cause too much stress.

But he loved the idea of owning that truck. In fact, he loved driving my SUV—he'd come by and swap cars with me whenever he was going out for pleasure or long-distance drives. He loved driving (and listening to all types of music—not common for a man born and raised in Italy!). He was truly looking forward to having his own brand-new SUV.

Several weeks before his last mortgage payment was due, one of my worst fears came true.

My father hadn't been well. He had pain in his chest every time he coughed, and it was getting worse. I look back and think I should have put two and two together … he often said how tired he was, but I assumed that was because he worked a lot and had bad eating habits (sometimes he'd go all day drinking espresso but not eating—until he got home at midnight!).

His doctor sent him for a chest x-ray, and later that day, I received that dreaded call from my mother: the doctor wanted to see my father right away. Even without knowing the results, I knew deep down that this was the beginning of the end.

Doctors tested the fluid in his lungs, and it was cancerous. Two weeks before his last mortgage payment was due, doctors diagnosed my father with terminal cancer.

My best friend was terminally ill. I felt like my life was collapsing.

Even though he paid off the mortgage, he continued to put off buying the truck of his dreams. He said he would buy it if he got better.

But he didn't.

He died in April 2007, without ever having bought the truck he dreamed of for years.

He had spent *decades* waiting for the "perfect" time, and because of that, he never lived his dream.

And although this particular unfulfilled dream of truck ownership stands out, it was just one of many situations where my dad was so worried about the future, he missed out on enjoying the present.

The truth is, he lived in a state of fear or scarcity, rather than in a state of abundance.

Because he had a good job, he was able to leave a small inheritance for the family, which helped us immensely during that initial period of grief. It also made me realize that if something happened to me or my husband (or both of us), we had nothing to leave our daughter—and if I continued to work for a corporate company, we wouldn't, no matter how much I moved up the ladder.

So, from the day my father passed away, *I made it my mission to cultivate an abundance mindset, so I could live for today.* I vowed to give my family the best life possible, now.

You see, waiting for the "perfect" day or time or situation is setting yourself up for failure, and you risk never living your dream. What if there is no future? What if the stars never align to create that "perfect" situation?

That realization, along with my seeing the limits of my corporate job—not being able to take time off when my father passed away, and limited potential for saving enough money to leave enough to ensure my own family's financial comfort—encouraged me to take the leap and find a business opportunity.

I quit my job and launched my first business: Virtual Business Solutions On Demand. I'd learned a lot from my dad, hearing him on calls negotiating pricing on his side jobs. Although he didn't have formal training, he had this knack for treating people like family and building relationships. He was smart: he knew that you have to connect directly with people who need your services now … not market to people who may need them eventually, or to those who have to be convinced they need your services. For this reason, he had a micro niche (he never used this terminology, but he created one just the same).

Also, of equal importance, he showed me that when you treat people well, they refer their friends to you. My dad never had to promote or market himself, because referrals came to him one after another. I think that's why I'm so powerful in sales and marketing.

Also, after my father's death, I bought his dream truck, to honor him. And now, my family and I live his dream for him. I know he's with us every day, living the dream, too. Still, I'd do anything to see him here, driving his own truck, music blaring, his beautiful smile lighting up his face!

It's my goal that in reading this, you'll feel inspired to shift into an abundance mindset, too … and that you'll commit to truly living *today*. It's my goal that you'll feel empowered to *create your own opportunities*, just as I did, and to begin taking action toward the goals and dreams that fuel your joy!

I've seen too many women struggle with their businesses, focusing on the wrong type of marketing (the type they see as "safe") and holding back on taking risks because the timing isn't "perfect."

They tell themselves they need to wait to launch a new product until they have a certain amount of income coming in, or they need to wait to invest in a course they really want to take until they have a certain number of clients.

The truth is, the timing is never "perfect."

There is always a "reason" why you shouldn't invest or launch or expand, when you're in a scarcity or fear mindset. (It's just like waiting for the perfect time to have children or get married or seek a new job. When IS that "perfect" time?)

But when you shift your mindset into one of abundance and take a leap of faith, everything aligns to support you.

As Mahatma Gandhi said, "Your beliefs become your thoughts, your thoughts become your words, your words become your actions, your actions become your habits, your habits become your values, your values become your destiny."

So it only makes sense that if you want to change your life, you change your beliefs!

It all starts with your mindset.

That being said, here are some powerful steps you can take to reframe your mindset and begin living from a place of abundance—where anything is possible:

Step 1. Practice positive self-talk. Negative self-talk can impact your mindset and therefore, your actions. It may convince you that what you want is impossible, and it may prevent you from taking actions that would lead to your dreams. Negative self-talk goes beyond telling yourself you're not good enough or not smart enough. It includes things like, "I can't change my product offerings; people wouldn't buy what I really want to sell," or, "I'll never be able to afford to start my business."

Action Step: Whenever you experience negative self-talk, reframe it into positive self-talk.

Begin by dialing in on whether your negative self-talk statement is true. For example, in thinking about the statement from above, "I can't change my product offerings; people wouldn't buy what I really want to sell," ask yourself whether that is actually true. Examine your answer, and then, shift the negative statement into a reality statement—and don't stop until you come up with a realistic statement! Consider this shift: "While I may not attract my current customers with my new offerings, I will likely attract new customers who better fit the product/ service I want to sell, and who do appreciate what I'm offering."

This will help you shift your thinking from a scarcity mindset to an empowered, abundant mindset. When you do, you'll begin to experience results that align with your goals and dreams.

Step 2. Create a flow of new, abundant energy by letting go of scarcity energy. Consider ways in which you can live the way you will when you reach your ideal state of being.

Action Step: Act in ways that energize you, and let go of the things that drain your energy. How will you take care of yourself (diet, exercise, grooming, spirituality, etc.)? Who will you spend time with? Which energy-sucking tasks will you outsource (admin tasks, accounting, personal, etc.)? It's okay to start small; make one change at a time until you feel like you're living in the state of your dream life.

Step 3. Surround yourself with people living the way you want to live. You're the average of the five people with whom you spend the most time.

Action Step: Choose your company wisely! If you want to start a business, connect with other entrepreneurs who have walked or are walking that path. If you want to exercise more, connect with other individuals who make exercise a priority.

Step 4. Create a vision journal, and begin taking inspired action to check off every single item on it! Your vision journal is a powerful tool to help you stay focused on your dreams and take inspired action to achieve them.

Action Step: For my step-by-step guidance on creating an effective vision board, download my gift, VISION JOURNALS: Manifest Your Dream Business & Life, below.

YOUR TIME IS NOW. Life is meant to be lived, so do it! Create incredible memories, for yourself and for your loved ones. Get clear on your dreams, shift your mindset, and take calculated risks now—or you'll miss out on opportunities and, more importantly, joy. Take a leap of faith, and the universe will support you. You'll be glad you did.

Serena Carcasole

facebook.com/amazingwomenentrepreneurs

linkedin.com/in/vbsondemand

instagram.com/amazingwomenofinfluence

Serena Carcasole is a Visibility Expert and a Money, Marketing, and Business Coach. She's the creator of the Get Visible – Get Clients – Get Profitable Blueprint, the CEO of Amazing Women Media, Host of Amazing Women of Influence Radio and Podcast, and Founder of the rapidly growing and in-demand Amazing Women Entrepreneurs Network. You can learn more about her here: amazingwomenentrepreneurs.com.

Download Serena's gift, **VISION JOURNALS: Manifest Your Dream Business & Life**, a vision board course and mindset bundle, here: hopebookseries.com/ytinserena.

Chapter 2

Meant for More:
How to Rise Above Your Circumstances to Create and Launch a World-Changing Business

By Tamica Lloyd

From the time I was a teen, the cards seemed stacked against me. Both my parents died when I was 14. I went to live with a family member, and things got even worse. Living on the couches of my friends and on the streets seemed like the best options.

It was the kindness of strangers—*and my own deep, inner knowing that I was meant for something better*—that ultimately helped me get to college and transform my life.

I was an angry person. I didn't trust anyone. People who claimed to love me betrayed me, and I felt unloved, unworthy, and ashamed. I felt like God turned a blind eye when my parents died and the family member I was placed with molested me.

This is also the time of my life when I began to put on weight. My subconscious was powerful, and I used food to medicate; if I was overweight, no one would want me, and I could avoid being hurt.

Still, I knew living on the streets was dangerous. I constantly had to watch my back. I saw the worst in humanity: beatings, thefts, and a lot of death. I knew I wasn't meant to be a statistic. I didn't want to die out there. I knew something had to change, but I didn't know *how*.

I had many angels during this time. One was the school janitor who let me take showers at school, washed my uniforms, and even gave me food to eat on occasion. He showed me compassion and *never* asked for anything in return.

My other angel was a Rabbi who often passed by on the streets. After a while, he started asking me questions: How had I gotten here? Why wasn't I with my family?

I told him my story: my parents were dead, and I couldn't live where I was supposed to. He told me forgiveness would help me heal and keep me sane. He talked about the power I had to ensure my circumstances didn't set my life on a permanent downward trajectory.

He introduced me to two books that changed my life: "How to Win Friends and Influence People" by Dale Carnegie, and "Think and Grow Rich" by Napoleon Hill, which talked about the laws of attraction and why people stay stuck in poverty. Soon, I began to practice what I read.

I was tired of being on the streets, and I began to visualize having a home where I felt safe and happy—just until I got to college, which was four months away.

One day, I was at a friend's house when my godmother and her friend arrived. They'd heard rumors about my situation, and after talking, my godmother took me in.

The most amazing thing was that when I actually experienced having a safe, warm, happy home, the feeling was the same as what I'd visualized for myself after reading those books. Things were looking up!

But then, at age 22, I was raped. I took an emotional downward spiral, and it worsened my relationship with food.

But I never lost the belief that *I was meant for more*. For *better*.

I started to practice forgiveness, just as the Rabbi had talked about. I realized I wasn't to blame for what happened to me, and I had to stop hating myself.

When I started to value and love myself again, things began to change.

I got control of my weight. I met a man I thought was a good guy. I got pregnant, and we had a beautiful baby girl. He cheated on me when she was 18 months old, and the relationship ended. I was lonely, afraid, and devastated. My subconscious continued to try to keep me safe … I started to use food again to soothe myself and ensure I wouldn't be attractive. My weight started to climb again. (The kind of wounds I was dealing with run deep, and my subconscious was still contending with them.)

In an attempt to get my life together, I swore off men, made a choice to finally get healthy, and went back to the gym. Years later, I met my husband, and life was finally GREAT. He didn't really care about my weight, and I let myself go. But, when I decided to go to the doctor for a physical, the results were shocking. I was considered obese, weighing over 220 pounds. I was diagnosed with Type 2 Diabetes (which runs in my family). My doctor basically told me to "live with it," and to get used to being on drugs for the rest of my life. This should have been a wake-up call for me, but I continued my self-destructive habits anyway.

Three months later, after receiving the results of blood work ordered by my doctor, the nurse called and told me to go straight to the hospital. My iron levels were so low, she didn't know how I was walking. I spent four days in the hospital, and received an iron infusion, which helped. After my release, I had to go back weekly for a month. The first visit was fine—the second wasn't.

I experienced a rush of heat as my eyes focused on the brightest white light I'd ever seen. I was having an out-of-body experience, and as I looked down at my husband and the hospital staff, I heard a genderless voice asking me questions. "Why should you go back?" "Why are you wasting your gifts?" I begged God to let me live. I didn't want to die, forcing my daughter to grow up without a mom like I did. I promised to help other people, if He spared me. As I was begging and pleading, I heard my husband's voice calling me, and just like that, I was in my own body again. I had escaped death.

Once I recuperated, I kept my promise.

I studied everything I could, like the China Study by Dr. T. Colin Campbell, and I implemented a whole-foods, plant-based diet. The weight started to drop, and so did my morning glucose levels. That's when I realized foods are POWERFUL. And I knew I had to share what I was learning.

I began the process of launching my coaching business. Along with my training (I'm a Certified Integrative Nutrition Coach and have a degree in Business Management), my gifts—healing, listening, helping people find their voice and take massive action to change their life—make me an effective coach.

It's my mission to rid the world of Type 2 Diabetes by reversing it in those who have it (or are pre-diabetic) while minimizing (or eliminating) the need for medications. I am also a big advocate of prevention, hosting classes for people who want to learn how to eat healthy and avoid this preventable disease.

I share my story with you as a form of inspiration. I want you to know that, no matter where you're standing now, *if you have a knowing that you're meant for more, and a deep desire to help people through your business, you CAN do it.*

And when you follow in the footsteps of those who have done it before you, you'll do it more quickly and more efficiently!

That being said, here are some of the most important lessons I learned and applied as I began building my business (so you can do the same):

1. Listen more than you speak. Not only does listening (truly listening) provide unlimited opportunities to learn, it also provides opportunities to connect with people—which is the foundation for any success in life. In so many cases, people just want to be heard.

2. Make a plan, or you plan to fail. In order to succeed in anything, you must set goals and list and implement action items to reach those goals.

3. Smile! You never know who you'll impact with a smile.

4. Be compassionate—don't blame the victims. Compassion will pave the way for those connections and for making the impact you're here to make.

5. Meditate twice a day for 15 minutes each time. Meditation is like exercise for your brain and can help you avoid stress and burnout. (Bonus: Read the book, "Stress Less and Accomplish More," by Emily Fletcher.)

6. Develop and follow a good morning routine. Before you pick up your phone, do things that will set you up for greatness. Read something empowering, meditate, have your lemon water, exercise … do these things before you start your day.

7. Develop and follow a good evening routine. Write about the good that happened during the day, the challenges you faced, and how it could have been better. Write out your intentions for the next day, including five to-dos. Pray, and read something that brings you joy before you go to sleep.

It's my hope that these lessons will help you develop and maintain a healthy mindset that forms the basis for your successful business-building venture!

Once you've begun your mindset work, it's time to start building your business.

Here are the action steps I recommend as you begin the process of launching:

1. Make a commitment to launching your business. Treat it as a business, not as a hobby.

2. Hire a good lawyer, or do some research about the legalities of your business. Obtain any certifications and licenses you need, and learn the laws of your state to ensure your business is protected.

3. Look up your business name to make sure no one else is using it. Most states have a website you can check, or you can visit www.legalzoom.com.

4. Create a business plan. Again, if you fail to plan, you plan to fail. Lots of plans exist, and the one you should use depends on a number of variables. A good place to begin: www.liveplan.com.

5. Define what makes you different. For my business, this step was simple, because no one else was doing what I wanted to do. My clients were desperate to get their health back. They were willing to try anything because everything else had failed.

6. Find your niche. Know exactly who you serve, so you can market to them as effectively as possible.

7. Know your elevator pitch. You should be able to describe what you do in a concise, powerful way, and quickly!

8. Outsource the small things so you can focus on creation (if you can do this, financially!).

9. Once you've done your homework, register your business.

There are so many resources out there for entrepreneurs who are just starting out (and those who have been in business a while). It IS possible to start your business, no matter what (I promise!).

YOUR TIME IS NOW! If you know you're meant for more, then I sincerely hope my story serves as proof that your current circumstances don't have anything to do with your future … that with the right information, passion, and support, you can do anything, including starting a business that transforms the world.

Tamica Lloyd

Facebook.com/coachtamica

Instagram.com/diabetescoachtamica

Diabetes Coach Tamica Lloyd is a Certified Integrative Nutrition Coach who is passionate about health, fitness, nutrition, and happiness. Her journey began almost a decade ago when she was diagnosed with Type 2 Diabetes and her doctor told her she'd just have to live with it. That wasn't good enough for Tamica. She started to read everything she could about food and how it affects the body … and she began to realize she may be able to reverse her Type 2 Diabetes if she changed the way she ate and lived. Within six months, her levels were normal—and she lost 60 pounds. Now, she's on a mission to help other women living with Type 2 Diabetes to heal. You can learn more about her here: coachtamica.com.

If you'd like help designing your purpose-driven business or improving your health so you can finally launch your business, contact Tamica to take advantage of her gift to you—a **complimentary 60-minute Discovery Session**—by emailing her at info@coachtamica.com.

Chapter 3

Build, Bound, Bounce:
A Proven, 3-Step Process to Make a Smooth Transition from Full-Time Employee to Full-Time Entrepreneur

By Michelle Clark

In 2007, I was working in the health insurance field when a friend offered me an opportunity to get involved with real estate investing. The real estate market was booming, and the opportunity was with a multi-level marketing company specializing in real estate education—basically, teaching people how to invest.

It sounded great! I thought it would be easy to make money, since everybody seemed to want to get into real estate, but no one knew how. And the timing couldn't have been better (or so I thought).

After a couple of months, I quit my full-time job (before ever making a penny from the new business), thinking I'd be making money hand over fist in no time, and that if I could just work on the business all day every day, it would come even faster. For the next six months, I did everything I could to get the business off the ground, literally investing tens of thousands of dollars in the business and in coaching, working hard to make it a success.

Then, the real estate market tanked … and the business tanked right along with it.

I was left with an interest-only mortgage, a large student loan I'd taken out to learn how to do the investing, and medical bills from an unexpected surgery when I had no health insurance.

Rock bottom finally hit in January 2009 when I filed for bankruptcy. I felt like I had truly, significantly failed. I'd wanted so badly to make that business venture work, and I'd thought that if I left my job and really hustled, it would. But I was also working from a place of desperation. I had no money coming in and was robbing Peter to pay Paul every month. Filing for bankruptcy made me feel like a fool: I'd fallen for a business scheme that was doomed from the beginning, and I was paying dearly for my misguided ambition.

After filing, I swore to myself I was going to change my ways. I made the decision to get back in control of my finances. I took on a full-time job again. I hustled to earn more at each new company I went to, and I got a roommate to help with the bills while I paid off the student loan that wasn't written off in the bankruptcy.

I started tracking every aspect of my money and paid close attention to the decisions I was making that would affect my finances. In order to get myself out of that mess, I had to figure out what got me into it in the first place.

Slowly but surely, I got back on my feet. Now, I'm building a new business I can be proud of—one that's entirely dependent upon me and my skills. This time, though, I'm keeping in mind the lessons I learned: I'm being patient as I prepare a seamless transition from employee to entrepreneur, running a business designed to help women transform their mindset around money and their approach to money management.

When I made the decision to start my new business, I did so with the intent that it would be in addition to my full-time job—not in place of it. And while my intentions have evolved (I am now working toward making this business my primary, full-time gig), I also know I won't leave my day job until my business is viable and consistently profitable.

I never again want to be in the financial position I found myself in with the real estate gig: a place of desperation, feeling pressured to make sales or hustle my income. No one will respond to what I put out there if I come from a place of desperation. And the same goes for you.

That's what I would love for you to take away from my story:

When you're starting something new, be patient! "It's going to grow as it goes."

Don't jump too quickly from your day job into a new business venture until you know whether it's a money maker and you have what it takes to make it a success. Give it the time it needs to grow and give yourself the time you need to learn what you need to learn. Which brings me to my three-step process to transition from employee to entrepreneur: **Build, Bound, and Bounce.**

Step 1: Build Your Foundation. There is a good deal of "pre-work" necessary if you want to create and build a solid business. First, get really clear on the type of business you're creating, and whether it requires physical products and/or your own time (like service, coaching, and consulting). Next, determine how much money you need to save to make ends meet when you do leave your job (typically, it's a year's worth of expenses, unless you don't need your income to pay the bills). This money comes in handy as you transition from a steady paycheck provided by someone else to a paycheck provided by loyal customers and clients. It's there if you need it, and it eliminates the desperation factor! Then, determine your startup costs and which prerequisites you need in place (social media accounts, a logo, website, a business email address, a business entity—like an LLC). From there, identify your ideal client and immerse yourself in the industry so you can discover what you don't know—and learn it. Finally, create a business plan with SMART goals. Then, talk it up! Tell everyone you can about your new business. This will open doors for you before you even launch.

Step 2: Bound into a Viable Business. It's time to get intentional. The best position to be in is one of control, knowing you have something valuable to offer, so that even if now isn't the right time for a customer to buy your product or service, you feel good about giving her the space to decide and possibly come back to you later. Construct your offerings or products, launch your business, and create momentum through consistent marketing, sales, and growth. Take care of yourself, too, so you don't get overwhelmed (money pressure results in no sales, and time pressure results in exhaustion). Put in place the structures that will allow you to enjoy the balance entrepreneurship can offer! Schedule in fun and down time and get enough sleep. Remember: the exchange of money between two people creates energy, which fuels your business and life. As you begin (and continue) to accept money from happy customers or clients, say a word of thanks and respect the dollars for what they're providing you.

Step 3: Bounce from Your Job. The timing is right when you have a steady stream of income from your new business, but you know you can't expand beyond that income level unless you devote more time to growing it. Adopt a "now or never" attitude, because if you don't, you may end up talking yourself out of bouncing, or it'll be easy for others to deter you. Take advantage of all the foundational work you've put in and the momentum you've created, and then… bounce!

When you develop and follow a transition plan based on my Build, Bound, Bounce process, you'll have everything you need to make a seamless transition from full-time employee to full-time entrepreneur!

I've put together some exercises for you to go through for each of the stages above.

During the Build Phase:

1. Do a Google search for the product or type of solution your business provides, so you know whether you're the first and only to market, or if there are others who are already doing what you're doing. And if there are others, remember we can all thrive, even amongst competition. Each of us has something unique to offer. Get to know your market size and the potential for making the living you're striving for.

2. Read, listen to, and watch everyone and everything related to your industry and building a business. Take note of what you learn and what you like or don't like about others in your industry. This will help you decide how to make your business unique.

3. Create a budget based on minimum expected monthly expenses, and then put it into action to see if you can truly live on what you've allotted. If you can, begin setting aside money each month—putting the difference between what you're spending now, and that minimum expected budget, into a high-yield savings account.

4. Set a date or dollar amount saved for when you will be ready to BOUNCE!

During the Bound Phase:

1. Use a calendar to schedule blocks of time (outside your day job) to focus on each area of your business every week: networking, marketing, blog- and article-writing, social media posts, refining products and offers, and serving clients or customers. It's so easy to become overwhelmed with everything you have on your plate that you can procrastinate yourself right out of success; that's why it's so important to create a system for devoting time, energy, and brainpower to your business.

2. Create, revise and perfect (at least for now!) your offerings. Consider doing some low-cost or pro-bono work to get the experience and testimonials for when you officially launch.

3. Learn the technology side of running a business—from social media to videos and audio, to the tools of the trade like email marketing platforms and SEO. BONUS TIP: Don't invest tons of dollars into software! Find free options to get you started. It's easy to get sidetracked with fancy tools but keep it simple in the beginning.

During the Bounce Phase:

1. Determine whether you need to devote more of your own hours to growing the business, or if it's a matter of hiring a part-or-full-time assistant to take on some of the tasks that simply eat up your time. Sometimes keeping your employee compensation coming in a bit longer can create even more of a cushion to hire someone else to do the work you don't need to (like administrative tasks), allowing you to focus on creating even more long-term business income.

2. Forecast where your income will be coming from during the next three, six, and twelve months, and be realistic. If you budgeted for minimum expenses, have you stuck to the budget? Would you need to add in the expense of benefits (such as medical, dental, life, or disability insurance) you'll be leaving behind when you're no longer an employee? Do you have recurring income from current clients that you know you can count on? Are there new products or services you'll be able to launch in the next three to six months that will create new income streams? Take a realistic look at how consistent your cashflow has been and also take into account business expenses you know will be coming in.

YOUR TIME IS NOW! When you follow this powerful, three-step process, you'll find that the transition from full-time employee to full-time entrepreneur feels seamless. You'll be able to operate your business from a place of service and abundance rather than from a place of scarcity and desperation. When this happens, you activate the Law of Attraction, and opportunities will flow to you! Remember, be patient. You're setting yourself up for success as you begin building the foundation of your dream business.

Michelle Clark

facebook.com/shakeyourmoneytree

instagram.com/michellemclark

Michelle Clark is the founder of Shake Your Money Tree, a financial wellness consulting and coaching company focused on improving financial literacy through employer-based workshops and individual coaching. She aims to help clients achieve financial wellbeing using her Seven Pillars of Well-th™ model, so they can feel confident and competent with managing their money, and without feeling stressed out or overwhelmed. You can learn more about her here: shakeyourmoneytree.com.

Download Michelle's free gift, her accompanying **"Build, Bound, Bounce Checklist"** here: hopebookseries.com/ytinmichelle

Chapter 4

The Power of Starting Over

By Jana Short

"Do something now. If not you, who? If not here, where? If not now, when?" - Theodore Roosevelt

How many times have you heard or seen those words, and let them slip right past you? Quoted from Roosevelt's call to action to our country, I've read them so many times on social media. I love beautiful quotes, but never have I changed my entire life because of one… until recently!

I was a (very young) single Mom until my daughter turned seven. I managed to finish school and then work three jobs as I struggled to do what you might be doing right now—trying to keep ahead of the bills. You know that other saying, about how "most people are just two paychecks away from being out on the streets"? Well, for me, it was more like of a paycheck-to-paycheck situation. No shame in being a single Mom and doing the best you can, right?

Despite working in so many different types of jobs for basic survival, my dream job was to be an interior designer. Being one to go after my dreams, I eventually (finally) managed to achieve it … which brings me to one more well-known expression: "Be careful what you wish for; sometimes, you get it." See, I was successful in my (then) dream career. I was able to partner with a great man in textiles, and he asked me to open a few "do it yourself" type design stores, where someone could come in, get advice from an expert (me), and do the rest him or herself. Not only were these shops very successful, but they also kept me pretty busy. But, because I loved creating beauty so much, I ended up going back out on my own. The only issue I bumped up against then was around creating professional boundaries with my clients.

Now, I am all about relationships and building rapport with my clients; they are all very unique and individual to me. And the ones who could afford me knew what they wanted and didn't care *how* I made it happen, just that I made it happen. I get it; they were paying me good money to make their vision a reality. Unfortunately, this created issues for me, though. I would receive calls at my home at 11:00 pm from clients who wanted to talk for hours about the shade of blue in their room. (Mind you, it wasn't even that they no longer wanted blue! They just now wanted a blue with two shades more yellow, and maybe one shade greener. I am not kidding; this was a real-life, two-hour phone conversation with one of my clients once, and was not atypical.)

On one hand, I thought I was accomplishing everything I had wanted. Dream job, check! Amazing client list, check! $500 an hour income, check!

But on the other hand, I was miserable. All the joy I had around creating beauty was utterly sucked out of me ... yet I kept showing up to do my job, and as I mentioned, I was successful.

It wasn't until nine years ago when I became quite ill that I realized I had built my business structure on a slippery slope.

You see, I was billing on an hourly basis. Well, when I got sick, I was in the hospital for six weeks, and my recovery lasted *months*. You can imagine what happened: the bills kept coming in, and I had no choice but to deplete my savings (that I had worked so hard for). Second, when I realized I wasn't going to be able to work for a long time, I had to find other quality designers to take over my open contracts, so as not to leave my clients "high and dry."

When I finally got back on my feet, there was no business left to return to. I also no longer had the heart to keep doing that job. My clients had built new relationships with the excellent designers I connected them with, and I was basically "yesterday's news."

I was 51, and had to start my life all over again.

What "saved" me—what completely changed the course of my business and my life—was my mindset.

I believe in pivoting … moving along with your current situation … and allowing yourself to be open to the possibilities.

So, I focused on what I could learn from my illness. And during my months of recovery, I continuously educated myself on holistic wellness and related options for regaining my health. I began sharing my story online; I became a holistic health and wellness coach, and later, NLP Practitioner. I started increasing my momentum, becoming the "go-to girl" for essential oils. (Essential oils were a massive part of my recovery, which inspired me to learn everything I possibly could about them and how they impact our health and world.)

I recreated myself.

That's not to say I didn't make every possible mistake there was to make! But I'll tell you what … I'm so thankful for that. Honestly, I don't know if I would have achieved the same level of success I have in the wellness industry had I not! "You can't become a diamond without a lot of pressure," right? (I told you I'm a fan of quotes!)

My point is this: even if you find yourself in a place of little hope, like I did when I went through my illness, *you can view it as an opportunity to move into something even greater.*

I not only LOVE my new career, but I am experiencing ever more success with it. I completely changed my world, and the course of my online business, by allowing my illness to open my heart to the possibilities. I became a massive influencer in the online arena, and I am helping others experience the same health transformation I did. AND, I have passed that love of holistic wellness on to both of my daughters, who are now Doctors of Natural Medicine, DNM's.

If you find yourself in a place of starting over, starting a new business, or building one you're already begun, I have some tips for you!

1. Share your story. Stories are compelling. They make us vulnerable, relatable, and most of all, approachable. Be honest and transparent (even though it can take years to build rapport and respect online, one small instance of falsehood can overshadow all your hard work and what you've worked so hard to build).

2. Collaborate with other experts. Join Facebook groups, and start getting to know experts in your (desired) industry. Connect with them. (I did … and I love Amazing Women Entrepreneurs and Health Influencers Mastermind!)

3. Look for author opportunities. When you collaborate with other authors to write a book, you reach more people with your story—and it needs to be shared with the world! This is a fantastic way to extend your reach.

4. Blog. This is another great way to share your story, advice, and expertise with the world! Posting blogs on your personal site is excellent, but you are only reaching your audience. Again, collaborate with others to get your posts on busy blogging sites to extend that reach. (I am partial to www.bestholisticlife.com, in my industry.)

5. Get visible. Say "yes" to summits, podcasts, and speaking engagements! The more you are seen, the more you develop yourself as a significant influencer. If you find it difficult to connect with people who have Podcasts and/or speaking opportunities, reach out in those Facebook groups and let people know what you're looking for. You'll be amazed at the level of support your colleagues can (and usually will) offer you!

There you go! My top five tips for extending your online reach globally, so you can be seen as a significant influencer in your area of expertise.

YOUR TIME IS NOW! Don't let age or circumstance stand in your way! I promise you, it's never too late to recreate yourself, just as I did. Yes, it may mean stepping out of your comfort zone. And yes, it requires work to build a successful online business in this day and age. Yes, you will likely have competition.

The difference between who they are and who you are is YOU!

I am the magic in my business … and YOU will be the magic in yours.

Jana Short

instagram.com/bestholisticlife

Jana Short is an NLP Practitioner and Wellness Coach, and founder of Health Influencers Mastermind, which connects real experts and major health influencers who offer their services online with their dream clients. She helps coaches increase their reach globally, thereby allowing them to share their expertise through speaking engagements, book collaboration, podcasts, magazine features, and contribution space in Best Holistic Life editorial blogging site. To connect and collaborate with Jana, join her on Instagram @bestholisticlife, or read more about her at bestholisticlife.com.

Get Jana's free gift, The Power of Your Story Workbook. It is designed to draw out your unique and powerful story, and explains how you can then share it with the world. Grab it here: hopebookseries.com/ytinjana.

Chapter 5

Start Living NOW

By Jackie Kossoff

I remember sitting at my desk in my corporate job, thinking about how the two years since college graduation had flown by. I couldn't help but wonder what I had to show for them. Staring at the four white walls of my office, I realized that I had always envisioned so much more for myself once I entered the "real world."

It honestly didn't make sense to me. I had done everything right nearly my entire life. I graduated in the top 11% of my high school (I was only four away from the top 10%); I received an academic merit scholarship to college; I earned two bachelor degrees in four years—while serving in leadership roles for multiple organizations on campus, including Student Government. I received a job offer one month after my graduation date, with a starting salary that surpassed those of some women I knew with graduate degrees who worked for multi-billion-dollar companies.

Just a few months earlier, my best friend from high school chose to end his life. In the midst of my grief, I found myself left with existential questions about the meaning of life and happiness … and I wondered if the path I was on lined up with what I really wanted. I felt something was missing in my life. It wasn't until I went on my first vacation in two years (a family trip to Hawaii) that I got serious about figuring that out.

Returning from that trip woke me up to the brutal reality that, if I stayed in the corporate world, my dreams of traveling abroad would either take place in two-week intervals once per year, or they would be postponed altogether until I retired. While I'm extremely optimistic that I will live until 75 (as a Millennial, I expect to not be able to retire until at least that age!), there's no guarantee my perfect health record or penchant for avoiding fatal incidents will persist untarnished.

And, perhaps for the first time in my life, I looked around me and realized how many people live decades longer than my friend had, without ever fulfilling any of their dreams. Like my coworkers—I knew most of them wouldn't exactly claim to be living the life of their dreams, despite having the college degree, decades of work experience, or the fancy titles.

There I was at 24-years-old, looking at my entire life spread out in front of me—and I wasn't looking forward to living it (or at least, the next 50 years of it).

If I'd already "checked all the boxes," why didn't I *feel* successful? Why didn't it feel like I was even on the path to success? Why did I feel so stuck?

I decided I wasn't going to stay stuck for much longer. I finally understood the phrase, "Life is too short!" It was time for me to *really* start living my life.

And I understood that, if I wanted my life to change, I was going to need to be the one to take action.

I decided to start with my job. I wanted—no, *needed*—a new one! I wanted a career path with more opportunities for growth and salary increases. I wanted more paid time off and a company culture that valued having lives outside of the office.

So, I began applying for jobs with complete confidence that I would find something just as quickly as I had the first time around.

One month and 30 resumes later, I hadn't heard back from a single company! Not even for an initial phone interview.

I decided to invest in a career and job-hunting coach, and ironically, that very same day, I happened upon a blog article while scrolling through Facebook that led me to the next step on my path to owning a business.

I read about two young women, just a couple years older than me, who decided to leave their corporate jobs and start their own businesses while traveling the world. I was so inspired! Their story made me feel like *anything* really was possible. Unlike the thoughts that came to mind while reading through job descriptions, as I was reading their story, I thought to myself, "Wow! I wish I could do that!"

I joined their Facebook group, and every day, I read posts from other women in that group who had left their 9-5 jobs, started their own businesses, and bought one-way tickets to the other side of the globe. I had never been so inspired by so many "ordinary" people before in my entire life! These were women just like me, who had recently graduated, started corporate jobs, and then, upon deciding on making a change in service of their dreams, did so.

As I continued following their stories, my awe and envy turned into sincere admiration, and I began to see the parallels between their backgrounds and my own. Many of them had worked in marketing, just like me. They took their knowledge of digital marketing and design, started their own businesses, and offered the exact same services I provided for my employer for their clients. My thoughts of "I wish I could do that," began to turn into "If they can do it, so can I." My mindset was shifting, and in truth, I was utterly terrified.

Now, as a practical person, I take pride in my rationality. I knew I needed a j-o-b to continue paying the bills, so I decided to take things slow. I could keep my desk job *and* dip my feet into entrepreneurship by starting a side-hustle. I was so excited by this prospect that I designed my first website in one weekend!

Before reaching this exact crossroads, I had never thought of myself as an entrepreneur. In fact, despite my degree in Creative Writing, I didn't really like the word "entrepreneur," because I tended to misspell it! So there I was, feeling my entire identity shifting, and I didn't know what to do about it.

I struggled with myself for several weeks. I felt like I didn't know who I was or what I wanted anymore. I was realizing that the life I *thought* I wanted, the life society expects us all to crave, wasn't all it was cracked up to be. My entire world view was shifting quickly, and I was frightened by how jarring it all felt.

It was around this time that I lashed out at my career and job-hunting coach during one of our calls, answering her simple question of how my job search was progressing by insisting I *didn't* want to become an entrepreneur. I must have continued for several minutes, because she ultimately had to stop me and suggest we speak again the following week.

Shortly after that incident, I realized how passionately the seed of entrepreneurial dreams had blossomed within me. It *had* grown too big to ignore; it was tearing me apart inside and making me act out in uncharacteristic ways.

There was just one thing holding me back: the thought of having to move from place to place. Most of the entrepreneurs I had been interacting with considered themselves "digital no-mads": freelance or contract workers moving from destination to destination with no home base. Although I wanted to travel more frequently, I still wanted Los Angeles to be my home, so I could remain close to my family and friends.

Then, much like the day I found the blog article that started my whole journey into entrepreneurship, I came across an arti-cle on Facebook about another young woman—one who was actually an entire year younger than me—who had started her own business right out of college and generated over six-figures in revenue in just 18 months. She traveled the globe regular-ly, managing her business from *anywhere* with Wi-Fi, all while maintaining a home base of her own.

And that's when everything finally clicked into place.

This was a business model and a way of life I could see work-ing for me! I felt as if I'd finally discovered the life I'd always wanted, without consciously realizing it really could exist. In that moment, I *knew*—intuitively—that starting a business was one of my life's callings. It didn't feel like a choice really; it was a given.

So I signed up for my first group business coaching program and redesigned my side-hustle website to reflect the new direction of my full-fledged digital marketing agency. I stopped applying for new jobs. I decided that I would grow my business steadily, perhaps spending the next six months finding clients and building my name as a Marketing Consultant before leaving the corporate world. After all, I had no time to lose! I had already wasted so much time in my j-o-b and in figuring out what I wanted.

Now, I still had fears. For example, I'm incredibly fortunate to be close with my parents, and I was terrified that they were going to disown me when I told them what I was doing. This fear was so real, I actually called one of my friends beforehand and got her to promise me her couch would be open to me if things didn't work out, and my parents wouldn't take me back in.

Like many of the fears that hold us back, this one was entirely unfounded. My parents reacted to the news with the conviction that they'd always wanted my sister and I to start our own businesses and enjoy the same freedom of choice they've had since opening their own law firm. For the first time, I realized my parents were entrepreneurs! Their support fueled my desire to go out on my own even more.

As the next few weeks went by, everything seemed to be going according to plan. I'd just signed my first official client when things at my 9-5 took an unexpected turn. I found myself with a decision to make—I could compromise my personal values and stay on, or I could take a chance on my dreams and dive into my new business full-time.

I decided to take the leap.

In less than two years, I went from 9-5 employee to full-time entrepreneur, matching my corporate salary my first year in business and fulfilling my promise to myself from five years earlier that I would return to Europe. *Now, I'm on track to more than double my income in my second year of business!*

There were only 90 days between the moment I decided to commit to starting a business and the day I left my 9-5. That's massive change in a super short period of time, right? When I think back, I honestly don't know if I would have taken such profound action to affect change in my life had my friend not taken his. In a strange way, I feel as if my journey is a gift of friendship between us. He helped me see what I was unconsciously giving up, and by pursuing my dreams, I'm able to carry on a legacy he didn't even know he'd leave behind.

YOUR TIME IS NOW! If you're clocking in and out of a 9-5, feeling your dreams slip further and further away from you, you CAN alter the trajectory of your life. You can pursue your life's ambitions, just like I am. And you can live so much happier.

Jackie Kossoff

facebook.com/jackiekossoff

instagram.com/jackiekossoff_la

Jackie Kossoff is a Marketing Strategist and Success Coach for ambitious millennial entrepreneurs who loves helping her clients create a life and business that reflects their own version of success! She is the host of the Millennial Success Stories podcast, and also runs a full-service Facebook Ads and marketing agency. When she's not working, she's probably reading, writing, watching history documentaries, or traveling to historic sites in Europe. You can learn more about her here: jackiekossoff.com.

Get Jackie's free gift, **"How to Leave the 9-5 in 90 Days Checklist,"** here: hopebookseries.com/ytinjackie.

Chapter 6

Breaking Through Barriers That Keep You From Success

By Elizabeth Otis

Whether you grew up around money or had a tougher upbringing, I want you to know that I'm not all that different from you. I have had the privilege of experiencing the best of both worlds, so I know what it's like on both sides of the financial spectrum.

As a child, I appeared to "have it all." My parents were married. I had great friends. I ate chicken nuggets every day. I had a pool in the backyard, and a friggin' ball pit in the basement! In my eyes, I had everything I needed to be happy. Little did I know that it would all be ripped away virtually overnight.

We had to move, and consequently, my lifestyle changed completely. We went from having everything we wanted (and then some), to barely having any food, let alone the money we needed for necessities … like a place to live, for example.

Seeing my family struggle ignited a burning desire deep inside me to find a way to make massive amounts of wealth. It didn't matter that I was a child; I was old enough to realize the difference money made in life. It wasn't long before my mom informed me that we had to move again—this time, to a place I hated even more. I asked her why, and she told me we couldn't afford to live in that particular apartment anymore. I was so upset realizing that finances were about to negatively impact us on a large scale once again. That was the moment I decided to buy my mom a house. From that day forward, I decided I would do whatever it took in order to obtain massive riches, so I could not only help my family, but also others in similar situations. I didn't want anybody to have to go through what I had been through.

Of course, that decision required me to *get my ass to work!* And I did. I ran lemonade stands and car washes. I went for long walks searching for coins on the ground so I could buy $0.25 cent string from the store. My sister and I would rally a group of friends to help us make bracelets from that string, and we would then go door to door with the finished product. I had the work ethic, creativity, and strategy, but it wasn't until years later in my adult life that I started getting true results.

Utilizing that same work ethic, creativity, and consistency I exhibited as a child, I worked 80+ hour work weeks in my sales and marketing job. I refused to stop at anything, implementing everything my mentors told me to do. Despite all of that, for many years, I didn't achieve *consistent* success. Regardless of the crazy amount of work I put it, I only experienced explosive little spurts of success, or "average" results. I literally thought I was cursed, because I swore I was doing "everything" I could.

For many years, I'd pound my head against the wall, pushing and shoving, consistently working and studying, trying so hard to get better. Yet nothing changed for me. I even developed physical and mental health issues, because I was so obsessed with hitting my goals that I constantly traded sleep and food for more work. I became so tired of grinding all day without ever truly accomplishing anything that I was on the verge of giving up. I was tired of paying for education without seeing results. I was worn out from meeting hundreds of people, but barely growing my customer base. I was so low in my life, I thought about suicide daily, and even attempted it. My relationships were poor. I was barely making enough to pay my bills, and I was bankrupt on every level: spiritually, mentally, and physically.

But I held on. No matter how tough it got, I would still rather die than give up on my dreams and the impact I wanted to make. I knew I wasn't cut out for the "typical" life, and that there was something more for me. I just had to figure out how to reach it.

It was at this point in my life, just when I needed it the most, that I learned the true power of a *Belief Breakthrough*.

Belief Breakthrough is the practice of identifying the deep-rooted beliefs you unconsciously hold about yourself that aren't serving you on a higher level, so you can completely demolish and replace them with much more empowering, driving beliefs. It is the act of rewiring your brain.

And that's SO important, because your brain is merely a tool. **It will give you *exactly* what you have wired it to give you—which is often NOT what you actually want.**

All the strategy, connections, work ethic, drive, and creativity in the world will only *help* you attract results. By themselves, they actually don't do anything at all for you. Why? Because the human brain is "wired" to avoid pain. So, if we hold a subconscious belief that associates pain with what we want consciously, we will never receive what we are after, because our subconscious will work tirelessly to keep us safe. This is why must first learn how to identify the beliefs that aren't serving us, and then start rewiring our brain for success.

For example, you could be an incredible artist with a serving personality. With your talent, work ethic, and ability to connect with people, you could thrive in your career—especially if you're implementing tactics proven to increase results. However, if something deep down in your belief system stands in the way of your relationship with your success, you will experience a very different outcome REGARDLESS of what you do and how talented you are. You won't see opportunities right in front of you. You'll accidentally say the wrong thing when you consciously thought you were saying the right thing. You won't accept an offer (even if you're broke!) because you might feel you "don't deserve that much," or the buyer "needs it more" than you do. The point here is that something will sabotage the outcome you want. It's limiting beliefs like these that keep us from receiving what we value or truly want and desire, because they contradict each other.

Events in our lives create beliefs that are hardwired into our mind, and they impact the way we view ourselves and the world around us. In my case, I grew up with such an intense need to get money that I had an equally intense scarcity mindset. I never felt like I had enough. Since I grew up around so many people who also had that mindset, my own feelings and beliefs about money were intensified as I bought further into their belief system. I believed "Money is the root of all evil," "Finances are stressful," and "I cannot do what I want because of my lack of money." While all these excuses seemed true for me at the moment, all they really did was contradict the outcome of the effort I put in.

Our minds impose limiting beliefs to try and protect us. Centuries ago, beliefs like, "I can't play around bushes because I could get killed" were legitimate, because there actually could have been a vicious animal hiding in those bushes just waiting to pounce. Today, we don't face those kinds of life-threatening scenarios on a daily basis, so our mind has evolved to trying to protect us from modern-day pain like judgement, finances, and love. If enough pain is linked to a concept, our subconscious will always keep us from obtaining a certain outcome due to that survival instinct. For example, how did I ever expect to make a lot of money if I thought it was the root of all evil? Subconsciously, I don't want to be associated with evil; therefore, my subconscious is going to create ways to keep me away from anything I consider to be evil … even something like money, which I so actively worked toward having!

Can you see the problem? Unless you actually value being evil over being good, you will never get where you want to be if you have certain beliefs, because your subconscious is the root to the fruit you produce.

So how did I do it? How did I ever get past the money issues I struggled so much with? I challenged and shifted my own beliefs about money. And when I did, I was able to literally make five times the amount of money I had been, start two of my own companies, attract the perfect people, and most importantly, gain back my happiness. I was already putting in the work … I just needed to change my belief system in order to achieve.

When we challenge beliefs by asking the right questions, we can begin to replace the barriers our subconscious has created for us with beliefs that actually serve us. I don't want to be evil; I want to be valuable to people. So, how can I challenge my belief that money is the root of all evil and replace it with a belief that serves me? Oh! It's simple! All I have to think about is what I REALLY want and am after. I value contribution, which is ultimately why I want the money. It would then be empowering for me to rephrase that belief into something like, "Money is the root of all contribution."

Take a moment to notice the feeling you get in your body when you say those two beliefs out loud. Can you see why you'd be able to attain more money if you subconsciously believe you are being more valuable with it instead of evil? And from there, you can re-program your mind with the new belief until it becomes as natural and easy as brushing your teeth, because it aligns with your core values.

Once I started to filter out the thoughts and beliefs that were not serving me and replace them with new empowering beliefs, my life made a complete 360.

Belief Breakthrough is a process that gets you to the core of your belief system: the place where your beliefs were originally formed. This is where the subconscious reveals itself, so you can truly break past the beliefs that limit you and step in the results you truly desire.

By monitoring your thoughts with the intention of correcting your language, immersing yourself in an ideal environment, and claiming affirmations with certainty, you can start rewiring your mind to achieve the results you want. The fastest and most effective way to do so is through a Belief Breakthrough. (And by the way, you don't just have to take my word for it. Many highly successful people like Napoleon Hill and Tony Robbins have attested to the power of it as well.)

YOUR TIME IS NOW! You don't have to wait. You don't have to struggle. Everything you want is at your fingertips! You're literally holding it in your hands right now, and it's time to step into it.

Elizabeth Otis

facebook.com/lizzy.otis

instagram.com/elizabeth_otis333

Elizabeth Otis helps people BLIVE by creating a life of fulfillment through belief breakthrough and energy mastery. She is passionate about teaching people how to create the experiences they so desire through actual science while enjoying every bit the ride. When she isn't working, you can always catch her doing something active to get her adrenaline pumping, or doing something to impact the cleanup of the planet! You can learn more about her here: elizabethotis.net.

Get Elizabeth's FREE gift, the **Mindset Programming and Efficiency Checklist**—the very same resource Elizabeth uses daily to turn vision into reality, and increase results quickly. When you do, you'll also get an opportunity to have Elizabeth walk you through her Breakthrough Process for FREE. Go here now: hopebookseries.com/ytinelizabeth

Chapter 7

Navigating Fear: To Leap, or Not to Leap?

By Julia Daubaras

"Wear something with colour in it; no patterns though. Something bright and lively. Smile in it, and you'll look great!"

This was the advice my mentor had given me as I prepared for a photoshoot to feature my new business.

It was simple enough, I thought. I was sure I'd find *something* in my existing wardrobe …

… or not.

All my life, my wardrobe consisted of basic blacks, blues, and browns. "Wear something bright and lively" was such a simple ask, and yet, every bright-coloured something I came across as I shopped made me cringe.

After purchasing a fluorescent-red tank I honestly thought I'd never wear again after the shoot, I told my photographer about my shopping struggle.

"What's your problem with bright colours? You look great!"

Standing in the busy street that was serving as the background for my photos, I felt completely out of my element. I was fighting the urge to half-sprint right back to my car when I had an epiphany.

I realized that it wasn't that I didn't *like* bright colours. It was that, when you wear them, you stick out like a sore thumb.

Have you ever discovered a truth about yourself that maybe isn't doing you any favours?

Yeah, for me, this was one of those.

There I was, trying to grow a thriving business, and I didn't want to stand out. I didn't want to draw attention to myself—to risk the whispered comments from people judging me.

In other words … *I was hiding*.

This got me thinking. Where else in my life was I hiding? And, in trying to hide … was I holding myself back? Was I missing out on making new connections? Was I letting opportunities to expand my business pass me by?

If I carried on the way I was, letting my fears get in the way of my goals … would I ever achieve them??

What I wore every day didn't matter to me all that much—but these things did!

The truth is, being afraid of what other people think has been a theme throughout my entire life.

And because of that, I've spent a long time leading my life within the bounds of what I deemed "acceptable"—confining myself to the expectations of the crowd.

As you can imagine, starting a business in that mindset—being so afraid of doing something "wrong" that I lived life intentionally invisible in a crowd—was not exactly a walk in the park.

In fact, because of my many fears, NO part of my business-building journey could be described as such. With fear always weighing me down, pressing forward was more like attempting to haul a backpack full of groceries and armfuls of extra-heavy (think multiple jugs of juice) crappy plastic bags that keep ripping on a bike through city streets while trying to go the other side of town.

Fear is *wonderful* baggage to tow around, isn't it? Yeah … it's been a slice.

But, as my constant companion for years, I've learned a lot about fear.

Perhaps most importantly, I've learned *it only has the bearing on reality that you LET it have.*

Let me share a story with you.

I am not a fan of bungee jumping. It's not a heights thing; it's a "the ground is too close for comfort as I go rocketing toward it headfirst" kind of thing.

So naturally, when I went on a zipline tour in Costa Rica a few years back, I opted out of the Tarzan Swing portion (a 100-foot rope they strap to you prior to your leaping off a very (read: *very*) high platform, that swings you like the legend it's named after).

I would normally expect a fairly even mixture of people who were and weren't going on the swing, so I thought I'd have the company of others who were equally not keen about leaping off a very (again, *very*) high platform.

The young guys lined up first, whooping and hollering all manly like as they jumped. Next up were some kids (kids have zero understanding of risk, am I right?), followed by those kinds of girls who only pretend to be terrified so they look cool, but who deep down are probably ballsier than any of the Tarzan wannabes who went first … and slowly, I realized that *everyone* was in line except me. *Not one other person* was backing out.

Not the old guys who were already aching from the zipline, not the mom who was clearly only there to chaperone her kids, not the Dutch guy who was practically crying during the zipline tour because he was so afraid of heights … not *any* of the people who had, at the start, casually commented about passing this one up.

I was the only one.

Now, despite having always lived my life worried about what other people thought of me, I have also prided myself on generally being confident and self-assured enough that, during times of peer pressure, I made my own choices. But something about this was different.

Many of us were visibly afraid. So why was I the only one backing out?

I watched that assorted group of strangers line up and jump off the platform, screaming their heads off (it's an odd experience when you describe it in words), and I began to reconsider my choice.

We were all listening to the same voice of fear in our heads: "This is unsafe," "You will die," "Why put yourself through this?" But each person on that platform was reacting differently to it. Some were pressing forward despite it, some were ignoring it completely, and some were embracing the adrenaline.

And that's when I had my "aha" moment:

Every one of those people were making the choice to jump despite their fear.

I was the only one letting it make my choice for me.

So I decided I would jump after all. And I did.

Sure, I was still terrified. But what exactly was being afraid doing for me? Nothing, besides making a decision for me that would cause me to miss out on an experience I knew I would never forget.

Now obviously, I am not arguing here that we should all stop being such wussies about clearly enjoyable and not-scary-at-all activities like jumping off very tall things with nothing but a rope to keep us safe (no, I'm still not into bungee jumping). What I am illustrating is that, far too often, we let our fear make decisions for us.

And here's the thing: the young guys who went first, whooping and hollering and putting a smile on everyone's face, and the Dutch guy who cried, and myself … we all jumped, and we all had an absolute blast regardless of how we each felt going into it.

Sometimes, even if we push through our fears and make decisions for ourselves, we still let the fear linger, making our ability to follow through that much harder (like with the crying guy).

However, when we let our fear go, our experience can be rich, and we can lift others around us up higher than they lift themselves (like the whooping and hollering guys making all of us laugh).

I'll say it again:

Fear only has the meaning and influence that you *let* it have.

Fear itself is powerless, except in how it manipulates you.

So how do we keep it from doing so?

Here's a little exercise I've used myself for years now to work through my fears. Ready?

Exercise: Working Through the Fear

Step 1: Think of the biggest fear or worry you have about a change you're trying to make in your life (maybe it's around managing your stress without easy-out coping mechanisms, or starting your business, or getting healthy/taking care of your body, etc.).

Step 2: Now, think harder. The thing is, whatever you thought of first probably isn't it.

Get really honest with yourself—what fear do you have that you don't even want to admit is there? That you'd feel uncomfortable saying out loud?

Step 3: Get quiet. Close your eyes. Let it speak its voice, even if it makes you uncomfortable.

Step 4: Now ask yourself:

What is that fear trying to accomplish? What is the positive intention that it has for me (i.e. keeping me safe)? Even if it has good intentions, is its presence making my life easier, or harder?

Step 5: Make a choice about how you want to move forward.

When you become aware of your fears and recognize *why* they're there by listening to what they have to say, you can then make your own choice about how you allow them to affect you.

And it's SO important, because when we let fear dominate our lives, we play small. We don't reach out for what we really want—what makes us truly happy. We don't share and contribute all that we could be, not just "with the world," but in our relationships with others, in our careers, and in our communities. We hold ourselves back from doing what it is that makes us our best selves. We hold ourselves back from what makes our heart smile.

If, right now, you're thinking all of this sounds a bit "woo woo," consider this:

If you're looking to live "happier" and play bigger, putting yourself in true alignment with what's really important to you … then this fear work will make a difference.

Let's go back to my terribly bland wardrobe.

Like with the Tarzan swing, my fear had been making choices for me. I wasn't only hiding in the way that I dressed: because I was afraid to draw attention, I was quiet. I'd stay in my lane. I'd keep to myself. I'd stay in my comfort zone. My fear of judgement hadn't just been harmlessly telling me to wear khaki (bet you've never heard that before)—it had been influencing me to hide *every* part of me: all the strengths alongside all my flaws. And that meant fear was influencing the outcome of my life… because I let it.

And that's the key—the reality is, *we have a choice.*

If someone judges you and says something negative, what impact does that have on what you do next? Only the impact that you let it.

As much as it might make you feel sick to step out of your comfort zone and set aside your fears, don't ever let them define your reality.

I have a choice as to whether I'll stay safe and hide, or play bigger than I currently am and go after what I want.

You do, too.

YOUR TIME IS NOW! If there's one thing you take away from this chapter, **know that you are in charge**—you are able to CHOOSE how you show up in this world, through failure and success, rather than letting the doubts and fears in your head choose for you.

Julia Daubaras

facebook.com/goodjujuliving

instagram.com/goodjujuliving

Julia Daubaras is a certified Life & Health Coach who one day realized all her least favourite problems in her life were being caused by (you guessed it) herself. Ever since, she's been on a journey to haul out the inner trash and live life bigger than the limits she placed on herself allowed—to live aligned with who she is and what's truly important to her. She brings this passion for living a full and rich life to her coaching, empowering women to take charge of their own lives by helping them create real, lasting change in the way they're living—transforming their habits and confidence. You can find her spreading the good stuff all around at GoodJujuCoaching.ca.

Get Julia's free gift, her **"My Fears Cheat Sheet,"** designed to guide you in taking action toward your vision in the face of fear here: hopebookseries.com/ytinjulia.

Chapter 8

Create Your Own Freedom:
The Inspiration and Support You Need to Build a Business That Supports YOU, Financially and Personally

By Tracy Meguire

Entrepreneurship was never on my radar! The very thought of running my own business was so far out of the realm of possibilities for me that if the thought ever even crossed my mind, it was quickly sent packing from my brain and my reality. I was capable of being a worker bee and nothing more … or so I thought.

They say, "Necessity is the mother of invention," and I guess in my case, being a mother was what sparked the invention.

Although I never felt qualified to be an entrepreneur, being a mom (a good mom) was the desire of my heart. In the puzzle that was my life, being part of a family was the missing piece, and I was determined to fill it. And motherhood was definitely amazing—all I had hoped it would be!

But over time, all the demands on my life began to take a toll. I was stressed, overworked, overwhelmed, and sleep deprived.

The joy of being a mom was replaced with feelings of obligation, resentment, and guilt.

On one hand, I was desperate to be the mom my kids deserved, but on the other, I felt like I had nothing left to give at the end of each day. And weekends, reserved for chores and housework, provided no relief. Something had to change, but I still had no idea exactly what it was.

Then, one day, the opportunity for entrepreneurship was gifted to me, through a series of events I had no hand in, and one for which I didn't connect the dots of significance for until much later.

So, it's accurate to say, when I first started my business, it was out of the necessity to provide for my family and have control over my life. At this point, I saw my new role as simply an extension of my previous employee/worker bee role. It was yet another j-o-b based on my experience as an accountant, which was all I felt qualified to do.

It wasn't until I began to understand the power of entrepreneurship, the ability to shape my business to be an extension of me, and to use my business to impact the lives of other struggling women and moms that my eyes were finally opened to the possibilities!

And, finally, it was in learning how to make my business profitable, efficient, and impactful that my entrepreneurial life became another extension of the passion and purpose of my life.

By no means is being a business owner easy, or for everyone. But I believe anyone with the drive to have control over their lives, be present for their families, be influential in the formation of their children's character as they grow to adulthood, should consider the benefits of being their own boss. Consider what it might be like to be in charge of your family's financial life, rather than at the mercy of some uninterested employer … of being able to set your own schedule around your family life instead of the other way around. Beyond even that, imagine being able to truly make a difference in your world in the lives of those you serve!

I floundered for many years, doing it the hard way and learning as I went. At first, I did everything in the business myself, and of course, it became an all-consuming endeavor.

But, over time, as I gained experience, I realized my business was an extension of me, and that it was another way I could create an impact in the world.

As my kids got older and more independent, I poured my energy into learning more about making my business efficient and profitable. I sought out others who were doing what I wanted to do.

My experience working with small business owners throughout my career gave me some great insight into what created success for some people and failure for others. I began to take note of which specific elements created a profitable business and a happy, satisfied business owner. I applied the principles to my business and began to see the benefits: my business generated greater profits, ran more smoothly, and empowered me to delegate more work to my team members. I ultimately developed a repeatable system to create a business that is profitable, efficient, and scalable ... a business that is lovable!

I now have the business I love; one that serves me, my family, and my tribe! I have more time to spend with my family and enjoy my life, but just as importantly, I have a way to give back to my community and make a meaningful impact in the lives of other women and moms to help them live life on their terms!

She Profits Solo is devoted to helping women design and grow profitable businesses from day one, and to help them understand they don't have to have big businesses to be profitable.

As a profit and business growth strategist, it's my goal to guide female entrepreneurs in the intentional design and building of efficient, profitable businesses that empower them to have time and energy to spend with their families and on pursuits that bring them pleasure.

Maybe, right now, you're considering becoming an entrepreneur. And maybe you're on the fence ... you're just not sure if it's for you.

Does the following sound familiar?

You're discouraged and overwhelmed, exhausted from being all things to all people. You're working for someone else, and you're tired and burned out and have just enough energy to cover the necessities (mustering actual excitement for soccer games, dance recitals, band performances, and school projects just isn't humanly possible! And forget FUN! You've got laundry and dishes and vacuuming to do!).

But …

When you think about the possibility of creating a solution, making a change, you feel *inspired!*

Yes, even if the volume of information and the staggering number of tasks seems daunting, you like the idea of being your own boss, answering to YOU, and being able to design your business around your life (not your life around your work and obligations).

And, even more, you like the idea of having the tools, knowledge, support, and confidence to create a business that's profitable and efficient, that supports you financially and personally, and enables you to use your gifts to help others.

If any of this does sound familiar, I want you to know—it IS possible.

It IS possible to create a business you love that is meaningful and allows you to parent the way you want to, to forge bonds with your kids and have the energy to enjoy that side of your life!

Because I know it might seem like a dream at this point, I wanted to offer you some steps to begin the process of visualizing and maybe even starting your business.

First, think about your answers to these questions:

• How much of your time away from work does not involve chores, housework, meal prep, doctors' appointments, and/or after-school activities?

• How much vacation time did you have last year that you actually used for vacation?

• How much time do you have to interact with your kids—reading, talking to them, doing activities together—during any given week?

- Are you able to volunteer for your kids' activities as much as you would like to?

- How much energy do you have at the end of a workday to spend on family activities?

Now, if your answers to these questions feel discouraging, do this **visualization exercise:**

Imagine you could create your schedule your way ... do your work when it's convenient for you and your family. What would your schedule look like? How would it feel to be in charge of your schedule, being there to pick up your kids, take them to after-school activities, and help them with homework? How would it feel to get everyone in the car without feeling like you're going to burst a blood vessel from the stress of rushing everyone so you can get them where they need to be, and then get to work on time? What would it be like if you didn't feel like you had to choose between work and caring for a sick child? Take a moment to really feel into this vision.

If this seems like a dream that will never come true, I am here to tell you that it can. Working for yourself, and building a business on a solid foundation, is not a pipe dream. It is more possible than ever!

Here are some action steps to get you started:

1. Figure out what is unique about you. If you're not sure what you have to offer, or what you'd build your business around, do some journaling about your passion, your purpose, your strengths, and how you're uniquely positioned to solve someone's problems.

2. Dial in on your "tribe"—the people you want to help. Who are they? What are they struggling with? Why do you resonate with them?

3. Get clear on how YOU provide a unique experience to your tribe in terms of how you work with them, how you deliver your services, and how to show that you're the only choice for your tribe when they're looking for the services you provide.

4. Build the framework for your business from the ground up to allow for maximum profitability, efficiency, monitoring of results, and adaptability. Once you understand how you are unique and how you want to show up for your tribe, it's crucial that you create a repeatable system to deliver on your promises. Your goal should be to under-promise and over-deliver, which good systems and processes will allow you to do. Good systems and processes also ensure things don't slip through the cracks or get done inefficiently, and you can train your team members to use those systems and processes, which gives you leverage to impact the world in even bigger ways. Also, it's important to have a way to measure results so you don't waste resources where they're not giving you a return on your investment. Measure everything: marketing approaches, operating expenses, hiring team members, etc.

YOUR TIME IS NOW! If, reading this, you feel inspired to become your own boss, share your gifts, and enjoy the freedom of entrepreneurship, then don't wait another moment! You CAN create a thriving, profitable, efficient business, when you have the tools and support to do it.

Tracy Meguire

facebook.com/tracy.meguire.1

linkedin.com/in/tracyrice

Tracy Meguire has been a financial advisor to women entrepreneurs for more than 30 years, and business owner for the past 20. She's seen what makes a business successful, and understands what it takes to create and grow a fulfilling business (rather than one that is emotionally and financially draining). Tracy is also a mother of four, and has always made her family a priority in her life. She's passionate about helping other women achieve the freedom and joy that come with owning a business intentionally designed for profit and impact. You can learn more about her here: sheprofitssolo.com.

Visit hopebookseries.com/ytintracy to download Tracy's free gift, the "Do You Know Your Profit Threshold" worksheet designed to help you calculate the amount of revenue your business will need to generate to support you.

Chapter 9

How to Bulletproof Your Business and Your Life—While Persevering Through Unavoidable Obstacles

By Lauren Cohen

This story involves a circuitous journey that began with a dream—the American Dream. Navigating the waters to my own American Dream has been interesting, exciting, and challenging. I share it in the hope that it will inspire other entrepreneurs … those who experience frustration at various points in the development of their businesses and consider giving up … because there *is* always a light. You can find the silver lining, as long as you persevere, stay the course, and remain focused on (and true to) your goals.

After I earned my law degree from Osgoode Hall Law School in Toronto, I realized I wanted to pursue the American Dream. I wanted to move to the U.S., but didn't quite know how to make it happen. When my husband (at the time) and I determined that we would have more opportunities south of the border, we consigned ourselves to making our way out of the cold via the painstakingly long and taxing journey that is the U.S. immigration process.

My dreams were short-lived, at least at the time. Just three years later, my husband and I divorced, and I moved back to Toronto. My return was not as easy as I expected. My body and soul had adapted to Florida's warm climate, and the cold Toronto weather was a constant challenge for me.

Although I'd landed a great job through a division of Citigroup, the "Corporate America" atmosphere wasn't a good fit for me. I took a new job as Managing Director of Legal at a Toronto-based mutual fund company. A few years later, when that company was sold to a larger financial services company based in Montreal, I was offered a choice: I could take a nice severance package, or I could move to Montreal to assume a less senior role in a larger organization.

I chose the package and returned to Florida to join my previous supervisor, who asked me to spearhead the development of a compliance business he was starting.

Since I was single, without any children, I was free to make the move. And the grass—and trees and everything else—definitely seemed much greener back in Florida.

It was February 2001. At that time, the startup world was thriving. We were optimistic and confident in the capital-raising space, seeking capital from all avenues—including my own bank account. I received a promissory note from my former-supervisor-turned-business-partner, a licensed attorney, for funding the loan.

Then, on September 11, 2001, the terrorist attacks occurred.

And the world of startup financing fell apart. Our attempts to finance our startup healthcare compliance company were not successful, and I lost my own personal investment. My business partner soon thereafter lost his license to practice law, and failed to honor his promise to repay my personal investment. This was devastating, as I thought of him as a brother. He seriously violated my trust and turned out to be someone completely different than I thought.

At the same time, I hit a couple other big bumps, not only on the immigration road, but also personally and professionally.

After meeting my second husband in Florida, he was "expeditiously removed" and subsequently deported by Customs and Border Patrol at Chicago's O'Hare Airport during our return trip from our honeymoon in Thailand. We divorced.

On top of that, despite having moved to Florida with the intention of practicing in my chosen field of law, my ability to become licensed in Florida and to practice in the U.S. was hindered by restrictions on my Canadian law degree.

Times were really tough, and I struggled to make ends meet.

But I refused to give up on my dream—my version of the American Dream.

Eventually, after several false starts, a series of opportune events combined with help and advice of friends and colleagues, and I was able to start my company, e-Council Inc. It was a single-source, turnkey concierge service assisting businesses that were seeking alternate capital from foreign investors, as well as prospective foreign investors seeking U.S. immigration options to find their way to legal status.

I found my dream in the form of paving a pathway for others to do the same. All my experiences—as an immigrant, a corporate lawyer, a business plan designer—and my business acumen and entrepreneurial skills combined to allow my business to flourish!

But I didn't stop there.

I wrote my first book, Finding Your Silver Lining in the Business Immigration Process: An Insightful Guide to Immigrant & Non-Immigrant Business Visas in 2017, and it quickly became an Amazon #1 bestseller.

Just a few weeks before completing that book, I successfully established my nonprofit, Find My Silver Lining. Dedicated to my father's memory, Find My Silver Lining's mission is to inspire and assist single mothers, working parents, and mompreneurs to focus on the bright side as they strive to lead fulfilling lives.

In 2018, I launched my second business, ScaleUP Enterprises, LLC. ScaleUP offers a single-source solution to assess and provide solutions to fill gaps in seven essential foundational areas, so as to ensure that the businesses are sustainable, scalable, and ultimately, saleable.

As an attorney, I've worked with many entrepreneurs who simply didn't know what they didn't know. They started up their businesses, filed formation documents with their home state, and then started thinking about revenue and growth. The problem? So often, they ignore the crucial importance of building a strong business foundation.

They cruise along, until something happens (and something *does* inevitably happen—an unexpected lawsuit, cashflow issues, insurance challenges, regulatory changes), and without proper guidance, their businesses can be destroyed.

Which is why I designed ScaleUP Enterprises—to guide entrepreneurs through a seven-point risk foundational inspection. It covers the most critical areas that could lead to business disaster, including:

1. Funding and Capitalization

2. Business Planning Strategy (including mission, vision, exit strategy)

3. Branding and Marketing

4. Legal and Compliance

5. Financial and Taxes

6. Operations/Systems and Security

7. Insurance and Licensing

You see, none of these areas of a business's foundation exists in a vacuum. To build a successful business, an entrepreneur must consider and address all of them to ensure each one is functioning optimally.

Maybe right now, you're reading that list thinking "Oh no. I am not an expert in branding and marketing." That's okay! Hire an expert as needed (and a small business attorney to guide you through the process of setting up your business), so you know your business is built on a strong foundation and functioning seamlessly.

Then, you'll be ready growth, expansion, increased capital, and a successful future sale.

Now, don't get me wrong; no matter how well you safeguard your business, you will encounter obstacles and roadblocks as you strive toward your goals. The most important factor in your success as an entrepreneur is your ability to persevere through those obstacles.

To keep you on track, here are my top ten tips for doing so:

Tip 1. Just keep swimming. Keep moving, always on the lookout for opportunities and trends, knowing that greatness is around every corner.

Tip 2. Maintain motivation and perseverance. Perseverance is essential. Only you can fix your problems. Perseverance goes beyond simply existing; it means being gutsy and engaged. So grab the bull by the horns, and don't let fear get in your way! Get some negative feedback? Turn it into a motivator. And always remember the power of support. Surround yourself with a team, at home and at work.

Tip 3. Work with a coach. Even the most successful people have hired professional and personal coaches—including Oprah!

Tip 4. Use every tool available to make life easier. Find whatever it takes to save time and simplify life. Whether that's apps that help you keep track of appointments, meal services, or online delivery services that allow you to order what you need and get it quickly, look for solutions that make your life easier and as efficient as possible. Again, hiring professionals to help you with the parts of your business that aren't in your wheelhouse is a great way to simplify your life.

Tip 5. Make dates with your family. It's like hitting a "refresh" button! Put technology away and use tech-free time to strengthen your relationships with those you love … it will make your business success that much sweeter.

Tip 6. Give back. Giving back helps you spread your message in a loving and positive way, so be sure to include a significant component of giving back in everything you do. As Winston Churchill is reported to have said, "You make a living by what you get, you make a life by what you give."

Tip 7. Build passive income. Passive income is the key to success. It will help you achieve your short- and long-term financial goals.

Tip 8. Always look for the silver lining. Every one of us will encounter adversity during our lives and in our businesses. It's just a fact. And in adversity, we should always look for a silver lining. It might be elusive, but it's *always* there.

Tip 9. Don't forget to take care of YOU. Prioritize taking care of yourself, no matter how full your schedule is, how long your to-do list is, or how busy you feel. Self-care is critical to your peace of mind, and plays an important role in your success, personally and professionally. Get exercise, meditate, repeat a mantra you build.

Tip 10. Nurture your spirit(uality). Set aside time, even if it's just once a week, to pause and reflect, in a neutral, non-judgmental way, on your recent experiences. Glean the lessons you can take away from your challenges and your successes. Keep a gratitude list and add to it daily, if you can. Focusing on the positive is a spiritual skill you can develop until it becomes second nature.

The truth is, **YOUR TIME IS NOW!** If you don't get your s*it organized, sh*t *will* happen—which can derail your plan and delay the NOW indefinitely! By taking steps to bulletproof your business and life, you lay a strong foundation for your business and persevere as you grow your company, to create the success of which you have barely dared to dream!

Lauren A. Cohen

Globally recognized entrepreneur and #1 bestselling author Lauren A. Cohen is an international transactional lawyer licensed in both the U.S. and Canada. Lauren is an expert concierge business legal advisor boasting a stellar track record of success. You can learn more about Lauren and her team here: scaleupcheckup.com.

And get Lauren's FREE gift, her **ScaleUPCheckUP™ Assessment,** to reveal the gaps in your business quickly and painlessly, so you can scale your business successfully without hitting roadblocks on the path here: hopebookseries.com/ytinlauren. (Use password a$s3$myBiz2019*.) When you fill out the assessment, if you reference YOUR TIME IS NOW in the "provide your business name and brief description" section, Lauren will also gift you a no-obligation complimentary one-on-one strategy session with her to help you address your gaps and figure out unique and creative ways to scale your business (value $247)!

Chapter 10

Your Message Matters:
Get Booked on Podcasts and Turn Targeted Visibility into Clients and Fans

By Sheila Galligan

My love for interviewing people began when I was a child watching the T.V. show Columbo with my Dad. In the show, Columbo is a detective. As he interviews people about the cases he's working, he kind of stumbles around. He doesn't *seem* intelligent. He asks "dumb" questions. And because he seems like he's clueless about what's going on, the people he's interviewing want to help him. They give him *tons* of information. What's so funny about it is that Columbo *is* intelligent—the whole bumbling sleuth act is contrived to get people to talk. And it works!

Another reason I loved that show is because I've always been innately curious (I was that kid who had to know why—why the sky's blue, why ice cubes freeze in the freezer). The standard answers were never enough. I had to keep digging.

Now, I've always been the shy and quiet type, but once I trusted you, watch out! In elementary school, I had a few friends, but many of my standout social experiences involved boys who'd chase me, knock me down, and call me, "Fatty." In eighth grade, boys snapped my bra. As I got older, I kept that small handful of friends, but I never got invited to parties or other gatherings. People made fun of me.

I felt trapped inside myself. I knew I had a lot to offer, but I didn't have the avenue to get it out there. And if I'm honest, it all felt pretty unfair.

Despite all of that, by the time I got into high school, joining the newspaper and yearbook staff felt natural, mainly due to that innate curiosity and my love of asking questions.

During this phase in my life, I was still a little shy and quiet. I still had a handful of friends, probably because making friends wasn't easy for me; I'm an introvert (which may come as a surprise, considering I interview people for a living—but it just means that I recharge with alone time).

I quickly realized, though, that the opportunities I had as I worked on the newspaper and the yearbook built my visibility, credibility and competence … and therefore, my confidence.

Through my work, I talked to the principal, the captain of the basketball team, cheerleaders, specific students at a school dance … people who weren't typically in my social circle, and with whom I probably wouldn't have spoken otherwise.

But I now had a purpose and a reason for talking with all different kinds of people, and this opened doors for me. I was seen everywhere. People started to consider me a friendly, competent person. I started to *consider myself* a competent person who had a mission: to help people get their voices and messages out there.

So in college, I double majored in journalism and mass communications. I reported on lots of interesting and unique topics and events, interviewing people in government, plays, theater. During college, I even had an internship writing newsletters for large companies. After college, I became a corporate meeting planner, and I flew all over the world, knowing I had a message and my clients were depending on me.

The bottom line: interviewing people brought me out of my shyness and built my confidence. It also added to my credibility—what I said mattered, as well, and people started asking me questions.

And that carried over into my online business.

Between 2008 and 2010, my life changed completely. Our country experienced another great depression as the real estate and financial markets exploded. These worldly economic downturns affected all areas of my life, as well as millions of others.

I lost my well-paying corporate job, and subsequently, my house of 20 years, for there were no comparable jobs available in my field. Depression and anxiety took over my inner core and decided to unpack and stay awhile. Then, the worst event of all, also in late 2010: doctors diagnosed my mom with cancer, and gave her six months to live.

She wouldn't let me visit her every day in the hospital; I was out looking for jobs and she didn't want her illness to stop me.

"But," I told her, "I can make money right here." And I made the decision then and there to do just that.

That's the beauty of the Internet: you can work from any-where, whether that's in your mom's hospital room, on a moun-taintop in Colorado, or at a lakeside cabin.

I created an "Online Office Organizing Day," during which clients logged in to my site and, every two-hours, I gave them an office organizing task. I also spoke to them through Skype and demonstrated ways to organize desk and email files, as well. I made $2K in a single day! I attribute the success of the Organizing Day to my experience interviewing people in high school and college—because I had the confidence to go out on my own.

And that event was the spark that lit my entrepreneurial fire!

I knew that, by interviewing people, I was able to help them build their visibility, credibility, and competence. I also knew I have a gift for asking the questions that reveal a person's special message, and for pulling juicy information from other people—information that showcases *their* gifts and messages.

I realized I was a conduit through which my interviewees (who otherwise might be shy and introverted like I was) shared their own messages.

So, ten years ago, I launched Go Big Global … so I could help people get their messages out there.

I spent the next eight years earning a living by creating vir-tual summits. Not only did this work pull me out of the dol-drums—the black hole I'd fallen into—but it also got me out of the house when I otherwise wouldn't have. I went to live events where Sandra Yancy, Suzanne Evans, and Lisa Sasevich were speaking, walking right up and introducing myself to all of them (and had pictures taken with them, too!).

The result: I was everywhere! I was credible. And I felt amazing … empowered and confident as I changed the world.

So many people have a voice that goes unheard. It's my mission to be my clients' lifeline: to ensure their voice *is* heard. So, in 2018, I launched my current business, Podcast Get Booked – Let Us Book You on Relevant Podcasts and Turn Visibility into Ca$h. As a podcast booking agent and strategist, I help my clients amplify their visibility, community, and income.

With the right conduit, you can transform your quiet voice into a powerful message for hundreds and even thousands of your ideal clients—by getting booked on podcasts.

Your message is important. Your mission matters.

And, podcasts are the perfect conduit for introverts to share their messages and missions. They're free. You don't have to be seen or do hair and makeup, or even leave your house. So even if you struggle internally (with anxiety, depression, panic attacks, fear of being seen, or any other struggles), you can still share your message with people who need it.

The best part: podcasts serve as an opportunity to transform from a shy and quiet person into the beautiful, outgoing, message-sharing person you are. You reach more people, with whom you build the know-like-trust factor. Your business grows. You change the world!

And as you experience that transformation, you also begin to experience freedom: more time with your family, greater financial freedom, and the freedom to be YOU.

I'd like to share a real-life story to illustrate what's possible when you finally allow your voice to be heard. One of my clients, April, invested in me when I started my business. She had a home-based consulting business, so she was "out there," locally. But I got her *out there* in a bigger way—in front of thousands of her ideal clients. I got her four podcast placements (gave her one extra), which allowed people to hear her interview and her message. She booked a couple of strategy calls afterward, and got a $5,000 client out of it. Imagine what would be possible if she did this every three months!

I want YOU to experience these results … to feel vibrant as you begin to let your voice be heard.

Here's a little exercise to get you started.

Exercise:

Develop a list of three podcasts you want to get booked on in the next two weeks. For each podcast host, create your "juicy podcast pitch" that will get you noticed. Write down what you will teach their community, and how can you bring value to their community. Include a list of platforms you will use to get the interview out there (podcasts and virtual summits work well, but there are other ways to distribute interviews as well).

Then, complete the following:

1. Write down which podcast(s) you enjoy listening to, and why.

2. Research! Find three podcasts your ideal clients like listening to, and write down why they enjoy those specific podcasts.

3. Leave a glowing review/statement/referral about a specific episode of one of the podcasts your ideal clients enjoy, including how it's helped you and how it helps your ideal clients.

4. Pitch the host: ask to be interviewed on the podcast. Write your pitch—detailing how you can enhance their listeners' experience—and get out there.

Here is a template you can use to do so:

Sample Pitch:

Hey Steve, I just listened to your impactful interview with NAME about why she feels so compelled to help people INSERT DETAILS. Your sincere and down-to-earth interview style really rocks and brought out NAME'S true "why." No wonder your show is in the top 100 of ___________ industry (or has X downloads per episode), and your community loves you!

Since you interview only the best for your thriving community, I would be honored to chat with you and share with your community how I can help them _________, or help them discover their_________ true "why," best exercise routine, etc.

5. Get booked: use my action guide, "Boost Your Exposure and Build Credibility with Podcast Interviews," (access below).

YOUR TIME IS NOW! It's time to go big! It's time to feel vibrant, to embrace the sharing of your message, the changing of the world, and the growth of YOU and your business. You CAN do this!

Sheila Galligan

facebook.com/podcastgetbooked

Founder of Summits Simplified and Podcast Guesting Prof-its, Sheila Galligan pulls out her personal Rolodex and books her clients on the most relevant and popular podcasts to reach their ideal audience. Since 2012, Sheila has helped hundreds of go-getter online entrepreneurs, coaches, authors, and speakers amplify visibility, community, and sales through the power of being interviewed. Personally interviewing over 250 global experts, Sheila has helped launch and manage Virtual Summits for top speakers such as Lisa Sasevich and Alison McKenzie. She has booked herself on 60+ podcast shows in 2019 and is shooting for 100+ shows in 2020. You can learn more about her here: bigpicturepodcasting.com

Download Sheila's free action guide, "Boost Your Exposure and Build Credibility with Podcast Interviews," here: amazing-hopebookseries.com/ytinsheila.

Chapter 11

If You're Not Growing, You're Dying

By Denise Threlfo

My entrepreneurial journey first began when I joined a network marketing company at 19 years old. To be successful, and following the advice of my upline, I placed ads in the local newspaper and did in-home demonstrations and presentations. While this worked for a little while, I certainly wasn't making the $12,000 per month that led me to responding to the ad in the first place!

Pretty soon, I soon found myself back in a j-o-b with boxes of product and promotional material cluttering up my garage space.

Nevertheless, I gave network marketing another go and joined another company. Despite giving it my best shot (again) with the abilities and awareness I had at the time, I never quite managed to "crack the code" and make a significant income.

My entrepreneurial spirit wasn't satisfied. So, when I became a mother to two beautiful boys, I chose to run a Family Day Care business from home. This allowed me to be with them for all the special moments, too, which was ideal.

From there, I started my own personal training business, which I absolutely loved, because health and fitness are two of my top values.

As you can tell, the freedom that comes with self-employment has always attracted me. Not to say that, as many of you probably know, entrepreneurship brings its own set of challenges.

For example, after completing my PT certification, yes, I could help people lose weight and build muscle, and yes, I could provide nutrition advice to fast track someone to success. But

I had *no idea* how to operate and manage my business! I was also trading time for money—sacrificing mornings and evenings with my family to train clients. And because of all of this, I ended up having to return to a j-o-b again.

Eventually, I recognised a recurring pattern in my life.

I would start with a company or a business, and before I reached any level of success, I would give up. I would see the obstacles not as hurdles, but as walls that were (in my eyes) impossible to get past. So, I would just give up and move onto the next project, without ever doing what needed to be done to break through the wall that stopped me. Yes, that's right … I would quit!

Now, don't get me wrong, I learned a lot from those experiences. But the truth is, *I allowed my belief systems to hold me back from taking massive action.*

I believed that I wasn't good enough.

I believed that I didn't know enough.

I believed that people wouldn't like me.

I believed that I needed everything to be perfect!

I also didn't foresee the struggles and challenges entrepreneurs so often face: the late nights, the overdrawn bank accounts, the marketing campaigns that don't work. And when things didn't work, I saw myself as a failure, so I would simply give up before ever reaching the gold.

The good news is, when I was able to recognize this pattern in myself, I knew it was time to do things *differently.*

The very first thing I did was to seek the help of a coach. Initially, I hired a mindset coach who helped me dive deep and discover just what was stopping me from earning the income I desired. She opened my mind to actions I could take immediately to allow in the abundance I knew I was worthy of receiving—the abundance that we all truly deserve. This was my introduction to the world of coaching and personal development. I experienced firsthand just how impactful that kind of work could be, and I decided then and there to become a coach, too.

Fast-forward a few years. I had once again been forced into working a j-o-b to make ends meet, when I started to feel that pull again. You know what I'm talking about, right? That feeling deep inside that there just *must* be something more than what you're doing? I wanted to make a difference to people's lives … to have an impact on the world!

I decided that it was finally MY time—and I wasn't going to quit again.

I followed my soul's yearning and became an NLP (Neuro-Linguistic Programming) Master Practitioner, mastering the skills of Time Line Therapy® and Hypnosis. Thanks to my own personal development work, I knew these were tools I could use to make a difference in not only my own life, but in the lives of others, too (specifically, in the lives of those desiring success in business).

My long journey into entrepreneurship left me with a question I often ask my clients:

What's holding YOU back from taking control of YOUR life and following your calling?

If, like me, that calling is to start a soul-aligned business that provides you with a "freedom lifestyle," you might be interested to hear the most common questions I hear from my clients, and my responses to them.

"I don't have a product. What would I sell?"

What if you didn't need one? Did you know there are companies out there that will pay you a commission to sell their products? (Even better, you don't need to store products OR pay for postage! It's true—they'll take care of that for you.) Finding a company that aligns with your values is much easier than you think.

"I wouldn't have a clue where to start."

Fair enough! Here's what I've learned along my own entrepreneurial journey—there are two key factors to starting a successful business: education and support. Yes, you need to know exactly how you are going to help someone, and what skills you have that you can share with those who need you. But you also need to know (to be educated on) the basics of building a business—whether that business is brick and mortar or online (the business portal of now and the future).

"I just can't afford it!"

This is your dream we're talking about here! Are you willing to allow financial fears to dictate your life? There are processes you can be led through that will help you find the money. (Really—there are!) You need to be willing to invest in yourself.

"I just don't believe this is possible for me."

This is where the support comes in—having the guidance of someone who's been there before makes all the difference in the world! The reality is that if someone has already achieved it, then you can, too.

The thing is, we *all* have limiting beliefs and patterns that keep us stuck in our current reality (even if we don't think we do!). The amazing thing is that you can rewire your brain so that you experience internal shifts that absolutely transform your reality.

"How do I rewire my brain?"

Great question. Start by asking yourself these questions:

What am I hiding from?

What am I avoiding?

What am I pretending not to know?

It may be difficult to face the answers, but once we understand our beliefs that are holding us back, we can start the work to change them.

And it's such important work! Because the path to growth will continue to bring up limiting beliefs as our unconscious mind brings to our awareness what is holding us here in the now and preventing us from moving toward our dreams. (Your conscious mind wants to keep you in your comfort zone.)

Now, once you've identified the negative belief, the next step is to face it head on, and practice the opposite, so you can conquer it. For example, if you believe that you are unworthy of love, then you need to find ways to love yourself from the inside. Once you love yourself, it will be difficult for others not to love you too, and if they don't, it won't matter because you already have it within you. You would have no need for external confirmation of love.

Next, notice the way you talk to yourself. Are you using positive or negative language? What we focus on expands, so focus on the good! When you notice negative thoughts coming into your conscious mind, flip them into a positive. Mastering your mindset is crucial. What we believe we achieve!

For example, instead of thinking "I am not capable of doing this," flip the thought to "I am learning to be better each day." Notice the physiological shift in your body. Do this with each negative thought that comes up throughout your day.

Finally, set some clear and defined goals, and take massive action! How, you ask?

Start by seeking the guidance of a coach. He or she can help you determine what it is that holds you back. With that awareness, you can then learn more about how to dissolve the blocks, thereby paving a much faster road to success in your business and life!

Believe in yourself!

YOUR TIME IS NOW! If you aren't growing, you're dying. Anyone can be successful online—from Instagram Influencers to 12-year-old kids crushing it on YouTube promoting toys! You don't need to have a business degree or even a huge following on social media to enjoy success. All you need is to break through the fears and limiting beliefs that might be standing in your way of getting there. When you master your mindset, you change your internal wiring, which is absolutely key to your success. Yes, hard work, persistence, and action are important … but not as important as the *belief* that *you ARE in control of your own destiny*. When you develop your mindset and internal belief system, it will no longer be a matter of *whether* you'll get there—it will be a matter of WHEN.

The first step: simply make the decision that you're ready to take action toward living your dream!

Your reality can change in a moment—the moment you *decide*.

We all have the potential to BE so much more, to DO so much more and most importantly to live life on our terms the way WE CHOOSE. We are born with a message to share with the world!

Denise Threlfo

facebook.com/DeniseThrelfoEntrepreneur

instagram.com/denise_threlfo

Denise Threlfo coaches women in discovering their message, developing their mindset, starting their own online business (even if they don't have a product to sell), and creating the internal environment that enables them to create aligned success. You can learn more about her here: denisethrelfo.com.

Get Denise's free gift, **a downloadable questionnaire** designed to bring you awareness around your limiting decisions so you can break free from self-sabotage, here: hopebookseries. com/ytindenise.

Chapter 12

Soaring Through Fear

By Trish Collyer

Fear—it can be a powerful emotion, can't it? Sure, it has a purpose … to keep us safe (think lions, tigers, and bears, oh my!). But often times, we allow fear to hold us back from growing into and reaching our potential.

I know I did.

I completed my coach certification program, and the additional (optional) training that followed. But I didn't feel quite "ready," so I found another course to take … and then another, and another. This continued for some time (three years, in fact), and even though I told myself each would be the last, I lacked the confidence to make it so.

My fear of failing, fear of being seen—imposter syndrome at its finest—was driving me to stay small: to continue hiding behind the theory that "knowing more means I can help more people."

At the same time, I really did think I was doing what I was "supposed" to do! After all, I was gaining knowledge and skills so I could be the very best coach I possibly could be for my clients. And I truly enjoyed the coursework, and everything I was learning.

But the truth is, fear was keeping me stuck. And I was letting it.

I remember one of the instructors of my certification program saying, "You will feel like you don't know enough. You will feel like you need another certification before you can get started … ignore this! You *can* start now." In hindsight, I'm sure he was right. But at the time, I was sure he was talking to **everyone else** in the class. I mean, *I* certainly didn't know enough yet!   (Why did I think I was different? Well, fear has a way of making you feel and think in ways that are not true to yourself.)

So, what was it that finally got me unstuck? How did I move past the fear?

My shift began with a seemingly normal conversation with a colleague, during which we discussed our goals and future aspirations. I shared my desire to start my own coaching business, but quickly backtracked with my well-rehearsed response: "I like my job, and I help people here, so I'm happy with that for now. Someday, I'd like to start coaching, but I wouldn't quit my job or anything." This kind of unprompted justification was standard practice for me. I'd share a desire, but quickly counter it before anyone could tell me I was daydreaming, and/or it would never happen. Usually, the conversation would then shift to focusing on the other person, and I'd be in the clear. But that isn't what happened that day.

This particular conversation completely changed my life.

Rather than passing over what I had said, my colleague asked me a question. "Why does it have to be OR?"

She had caught me off guard, and must have noticed, because she quickly added, "I mean, it sounds like you're saying it has to be one or the other … but could it be both?"

It suddenly seemed so obvious! Yes, I had thought about doing both at the same time before, but I mean, who has time for that? I caught myself before I uttered those very words in response to my colleague's question. Instead, this time, I actually thought about it. Next, she said, "Consider the possibility of doing the job you do now AND coaching clients—what would that future look like?"

That night, I thought about our conversation. I began by simply asking myself if I *could* do both. And I thought, *sure, I could!*

Then the next question: *So what IS stopping me then?*

And the answer hit me like a brick to the face: FEAR.

For three years, fear told me to "be better for your clients." But really, all those programs and courses (as beneficial as they were) had been excuses for me to put off my coaching dream. The whole, "I don't want to leave my day job" thing? Another excuse. And the thing is, these excuses *were* keeping me safe. *But they were also keeping me small.*

When that realization hit me, it was like a weight lifted from my shoulders. The knots in my stomach turned into butterflies! I was so excited to finally get started. Taking stock of everything my courses had taught me, it was apparent that I really DO know enough!

Still, even as the fear of not knowing enough started to melt away, another fear—that of being judged—quickly took its place. What would people think? Would they trust me? Would they laugh at me? I could feel the butterflies turning back into knots, the previous excitement stifled by fear, again.

I decided I wasn't willing to give up. So, in an effort to work through that fear, I asked myself, "What's the worst that could happen?" And then, "So what if they unfriend me? If being me and being true to myself is all it takes for someone to walk away, was she ever really my friend, anyway?"

And again, as that fear dissipated, another crept in … what if no one signs up to work with me? Or what if they do sign up, but I can't help them? But in that very moment, before I let the new fear take over, I talked back to it. I said, "Nope. Not today. I'm breaking the cycle. Fear will not stop me today!"

And in that moment, I knew. I knew I would never have all the answers. I would *never* feel "ready." There would be no "perfect time" to start.

I would just have to do it afraid!

How, you ask? Maybe you're thinking I'm different than you, and must somehow now be blessed with superhuman amounts of courage to keep me completely unfazed by naysayers and the opinions of others. No, it's not that … not in the least (quite the opposite, actually).

The difference is, *I shifted my mindset.*

I made the decision to do it afraid—no matter what—because if it didn't work out, I would at least know that I tried.

The truth is, most of my life, I've let other people's opinions drive my decisions. I've worked hard to live up to who others expected me to be become.

But there have been moments here and there when I listened to my gut, and did what I thought was right. And it worked out alright! Not without challenges, but in the end, every time I listened to my gut, I ended up being glad I did.

So where EXACTLY did I find the courage to be seen … to finally show up for myself?

I borrowed it.

A visioning exercise helped me move through my fear and take action.

I imagined my future self standing on a stage, speaking wisdom into a room packed with thousands of people so far back that large screens were set up for them to see and hear me. She was polished—professional yet inviting. The audience leaned in to her every word as she spoke with a calm confidence. Near the end of her speech, the audience had shifted—they were thinking (*truly* thinking). They were uplifted and energized by the possibilities that lie ahead, as they wondered how one hour could have impacted them so deeply.

Thinking of her, I asked myself what *she* would do in my situation. What would she suggest I do? Would she let fear stop her? No way, not a chance! The future me influential speaker would move mountains for the opportunity to impact the lives of others!

Then I asked myself, *what do I need to do now, to be her in five years?* The answer was clear—I needed to start coaching. And in order to start coaching, I needed to advertise (what? No way, that's too scary, I thought … the fear creeping back and overwhelming me).

No! I stopped my negative thoughts in their tracks. *She* wouldn't let fear overwhelm her, and neither would I. I refused to be the reason she didn't achieve her dream. I would not stand in her way.

Instead, I borrowed her confidence and decided to do it afraid.

As one of my mentors advises, I decided to "hold an image of what is possible."

Once I did that, I could then allow the image to guide me to my destination. And that is what I did.

With that borrowed confidence, I took one step. I offered my coaching to one person. That person believed in me, so I took another step.

And step by step, one at a time, I became who I am today.

I am still on my path to become my future self—and I know her confidence will show me the way.

Maybe, right now, fear is holding you back, too. Maybe it's keeping you from what you want most.

I've got you! Here's an exercise to help you work through it. (These are the exact steps I take every time I find myself stuck or trying to move past an obstacle.)

S.O.A.R. Through Fear

S – See it:

Get clear on what you really want. Envision your desired future. Visualize the next step you need to take to get you there.

O – Own it:

Own what has been holding you back. Own the fact that, up until now, you've let it stop you. Own the choice to not let it stop you any longer.

A – Action it:

Take action—just one step to start—to move past that barrier that had been keeping you stuck. Make a plan and follow through.

R – Reflect on it:

How did it go? What did you learn? What is your next step that will help you reach your desired future?

Working through these steps is a starting point in getting unstuck … in moving past the things that may be holding you back.

YOUR TIME IS NOW! And I believe in you! You wouldn't be reading this book if you didn't have a passion.

I encourage you to SOAR through the fear—don't let it snowball into an overwhelming avalanche!

Share your gifts.

The world is waiting for you!

Trish Collyer

facebook.com/WellnessWithTrish

linkedin.com/in/trish-collyer

instagram.com/wellnesswithtrish

As a certified coach, Trish Collyer's passion is to make a positive impact in the world by helping people create their BEST life. With a background in communication, personal growth, relationships, health and nutrition, leadership, and DISC behavioral analysis, Trish strives to support her clients in choosing greatness over mediocrity, so they can achieve everything they desire and more. You can learn more about her here: trishcollyer.com.

Still feel like fear is keeping you stuck? Get Trish's downloadable workbook, **Fear-Free: Eleven Ways to Overcome Your Fear,** for more detailed guidance in visualizing your future, identifying what's stopping you, and moving past fear here: hopebookseries.com/ytintricia.

Chapter 13

Pursuing Your Dream:
First Steps to Living the Life You REALLY Want

By Christi Davis

Looking back, it is clear to me that every road I ever traveled led me to fulfill my calling as a health coach.

As a teenager, I struggled with my weight. I had an issue with portion control, always finishing what was put in front of me. At 19 (after putting on "the Freshman 15+"), I started doing Lean Line (a program similar to Weight Watchers). It was wonderful, and I lost about 25 pounds. However, the struggle continued over the years to maintain my weight, and I was constantly fluctuating.

At 28, I received an absolute wake-up call when I was diagnosed with Multiple Sclerosis. Realizing the fragility of the human body shook me to my core, and I was afraid of the vision I had of my future. I imagined what it might be like should the disease progress to a point of limiting my ability to live the life I truly wanted for myself.

The fear of the unknown was terrifying. What if I were destined to live my life in a wheelchair, with my husband as my caretaker? Would my dream of raising a family no longer become our future? My thoughts spiraled. The concept of losing control of my life was unfathomable.

I decided a wheelchair was *not* an option, and made it my mission to get strong and healthy, once and for all (while staying in remission with my MS).

I began making changes right away, cleaning up my diet and exercising regularly. At the same time, my husband and I wanted children, and I couldn't start the MS treatment and medication if we were going to try for a baby. This meant prioritizing our family planning and waiting to start treatment. That's exactly what we did, and it wasn't until our second child was born four years later that I started the medication.

Having gained 60+ pounds during each pregnancy, my weight was still an issue. I decided then to get back in control, and learned how to manage portions and make healthy food choices. I remained in remission during this time as well, and soon, people who had friends or family affected by MS (and other autoimmune diseases) began reaching out to me. They wanted me to share my experiences with my disease and teach others how to manage it as well as I was able to. I was always happy to speak or email individuals offering that kind of advice and support.

Now, at the time (2016), I had a wonderful job with a marketing company. Despite having a Bachelor of Science degree with a focus in Nutrition, I wasn't living my passion to support others on their health-related journeys. So, I decided to dabble (as a side gig) in a new venture in fitness and health supplements (protein shakes and recorded video workouts), in alignment with my vision. While I loved the company, I soon realized that what I really wanted to do was to work more closely with autoimmune-compromised individuals, with a focus on improving their health with dietary modifications and permanent habit change. This experience truly helped propel me to become a Health Coach, and I am grateful for it and so many wonderful takeaways.

Time was passing me by, and I knew if I didn't start pursuing my dreams soon, I would be filled with colossal regret. It was shortly after my 46th birthday that I decided to take a step back to reflect again on what I truly wanted. I realized I wanted—*no, needed*—to fulfill the passion I felt for helping others get truly healthy. I had the education and the experience to do it (after all, I was doing it for myself, undergoing all kinds of successes and failures along the way). And I knew the right ways to go about being healthy, and was SO ready to work with others struggling with their own health to show them how they could transform it completely, and thrive.

Plus, to be blunt, I knew I didn't want to someday be on my death bed, full of regret over failing to pursue my life-long passion.

So, despite being right in the middle of renovating our home AND the busy season at the marketing agency (never mind the kids' demanding schedules), I decided it was time—time to answer my life's calling.

I had so many ideas for turning my passion into a lucrative career! Maybe I would start a healthy food truck. That could be fun! Or, maybe I'd start my very own YouTube channel focusing on healthy recipes and anti-inflammatory meal options. Maybe I would offer cooking lessons in my home! The brainstorming continued, but I had NO CLUE how to decide which to pursue.

I knew I needed guidance, and as luck (or fate!) would have it, that's when I stumbled upon Carrie Green's book, *She Means Business*. How it spoke to (and inspired) me! Carrie's work is in helping women entrepreneurs create their own businesses, complete with all the steps and encouragement, and that was the subject matter of the book. It was the perfect resource!

Shortly after starting the book, I received our County Night School course listing in the mail. I always wanted to take a class, but was never able to find the time to make it happen. When I saw a course called, "The Power of Food," taught by a very knowledgeable Health Coach who specialized in Integrative and Functional Medicine, it was a no brainer … I just *had* to take it! Taking the course made me realize three important things: first, that I really did have a wealth of knowledge already inside me. Second, I absolutely loved learning about ways to eat healthier and optimize health. And third, that *I had the ability to teach and help others.*

I knew beyond a shadow of a doubt that I wanted to be a Health Coach—I was driven to support people with autoimmune diseases (or other compromised health issues) by guiding them to healthy living (without feeling deprived or overwhelmed). So,

I began researching programs that could certify me. There are quite a few out there, and was set on choosing the one that best represented my mission. When I found the Health Coach Institute, I knew it was meant to be.

Once I started the course, I became relentless in starting my own business. I came up with my website name and creation, logo design, and business cards. I gathered recipes with images, launched social media platforms, and announced my business journey venture so everyone I knew would be aware of what I was up to. I was ready, and nothing would stop me!

Three months into the program, I already had my two "practice clients" started on their 90-Day Transformation Programs I had created for them. I also had people reaching out to me in person and via social media, inquiring about my health coaching practice. Soon, my website officially launched, and I was SO excited. It was ALL happening! I was like a kid in a candy shop, literally unable to contain my excitement. Even the MS flare up I was dealing with during this time would NOT stop me! I kept going, squeezing in recipe creation, website edits, affiliate partnerships, and so much more into an already jam-packed schedule. I was determined to have my business completely ready for launch upon my certification. And it was!

In September 2019, Christi Health Coach opened to the world!

And I have been living my passion ever since.

Working with clients and seeing their progress gives me such an incredible amount of joy. The little "aha" moments … the small changes they make that add up to amazing results in their health … I am completely in my element helping others improve their quality of life, and I couldn't be happier.

The message I want to leave you with today is that *you* can do it, too. You can make your dreams a reality, too, through entrepreneurship! And because I know how overwhelming it can feel to even know where to start, I'm sharing a few tips with you today.

Tip 1: First thing's first: you have to **find your underlying passion within.** What sparks your fire and gets you excited and provokes unending satisfaction for you? What would others say are your talents?

Tip 2: Create an action plan that covers all angles around turning that passion into a business. (From brainstorming ideas like the food truck, to conducting research.) Create an outline mapping this into a business. From there start filling in the details through detailed research.

Tip 3: Start talking/networking with those already in the field. Establishing a mentor already in the field can set you up for success. You can find others via social media groups who are in the industry. You can mutually benefit from each other's experiences. I learned so much from my now colleagues! I reached out to them, listened attentively, and took tons of notes. I also learned that getting several perspectives helped obtain critical points from each individual. Each individual's experience was unique while offering awesome feedback that I could apply to my business.

Tip 4: When you begin marketing and creating your social media platforms, **stay consistent!** Find ways to keep everything cohesively fresh while incorporating repetitive information. This helps make the information you are providing stick with your audience. Having a specialty/niche is also instrumental. When people can relate to your area of expertise, you have an audience that wants more. From here, you will see your business grow!

Tip 5: Keep a positive mindset—yes, this is a tricky one at times. Just when you think no one is hearing your message, or responding to your offers, or "liking" your posts, you'll run into someone who tells you how much what you are doing means. How you speak directly to him or her, and s/he truly resonates.

And you know you are making a difference. Your passion now has purpose!

Maybe right now, you're thinking "Ugh … that sounds like so much work." I'll tell you this: hard work does not *feel* like work when you're making your dreams come to fruition! Just wait and see.

YOUR TIME IS NOW! When you fuel your dreams with your passion and desire to succeed, you set yourself up for inevitable success!

Christi Davis

facebook.com/christihealthcoach

Christi Davis, founder of Christi Health Coach, is a self-proclaimed "nutrition nerd." Certified Health Coach through the Health Coach Institute (accredited through the International Coaching Federation), she specializes in autoimmune wellness, helping people reclaim their energy and confidence in the face of health challenges while guiding them in living their absolute best life. Join her private Facebook group—Autoimmune Wellness and Whole Body Nutrition—for tips, recipes, and challenges. Learn more about her here: christihealthcoach.com.

And, get Christi's free gift, her **Autoimmune Friendly Cookbook**, consisting of 15 flavor-packed, autoimmune-friendly recipes that will please your family and friends, too! hopebookseries.com/ytinchristi

Chapter 14

Navigating the Bridges of Your Life

By Deni Carruth

There I was, sitting on the floor, legs spread, doing gentle stretches to ease my low back pain before getting ready for work (something I did *not* look forward to). Suddenly, like a switch, my back completely locked up. Any attempt to move was excruciating. I was home alone, and fear set in quickly. As soon as I was able, I crawled to the "wall phone" (yes, it was that long ago) and held tight to the cord as I inched my way up the wall to the best standing position I could manage. I called my husband in a panic, and he came home to take me to the doctor.

There was no changing of clothes. Every movement took so much effort. Every step hurt. Every breath was shallow. I was doing all that I knew how to prevent a muscle spasm, because I knew what could come next. My thoughts were just creating more tension, and my body was becoming more and more rigid.

Have you ever tried to get in and out of a car while moving your body as little as possible? Yeah. I can't tell you how many times my breath just stopped from the pain, which in turn caused more tension.

The x-ray revealed the "normal" misalignment in my spine that resulted from a car accident I was in with my sister back in high school. My doctor asked, "Are you under any stress?"

Ha! I immediately thought of my job. I enjoyed what I did as an admin and co-editor for a magazine, but the man I worked for was … I'll just leave it there.

For two years previous, I had held various jobs that took a toll on my mind, body, and spirit, and there I was again, stuck in a chronic pain saga: That "toll" was causing stress. The stress was causing tension in my body. The tension was causing muscle spasms. The muscle spasms were worsening the misalignment. And unfortunately, the entire cycle had become painfully familiar.

The doctor prescribed muscle relaxers, ordered me to lay flat on my back on ice for a week, and cautioned me to lessen the stress in my life. (*Right*, I thought. *No problem.*)

I knew something had to change.

I soon left that job and acquired a position as administrative secretary to four hospital administrators. It was there that I came upon a great opportunity to take advantage of aerobics classes offered at the hospital for employees. Since it was taught by a nurse who worked there, it seemed safe enough to me, and I hoped to maybe even get some help in moving better with less pain.

After my first class (which was also the only one I took), I commented to the nurse instructor that I had experienced some level of pain during most movements and asked for modifications. Her response was not new to me. "If it hurts, don't do it." Maybe you've heard that before, too? Maybe you've felt the disappointment I felt when I thought, *"If I don't do what hurts, I'll do almost nothing!"* I was at my end with that mindset. I knew that doing nothing was doing nothing for me.

Fast forward to a job relocation for my husband. I had mixed feelings about the move. Our marriage wasn't the best then, and I would be moving away from family again.

Stress.

There I stood, facing a life change filled with uncertainty and pain. Mind. Body. Spirit. I couldn't help but wonder when it would be *my* turn. When would I go through a change that was for ME … first? Sounds selfish, maybe … but if you're honest with yourself, and dig deep, I think you might be able to relate.

I was facing what seemed at the time to be a long, scary, uncertain bridge. But I knew I wanted a better marriage, a better body, and a better me. I knew I wanted to get to a better place.

So I started the journey across.

In our new location, I was on a mission (and because I wasn't initially working, I could focus on it). I was determined to find a way to not just exercise, but move without pain, because that feeling of being locked up in my body was showing up in other areas of my life. (Or was it the other way around?)

I knew two things for sure:

1. God created my body, me, for movement.

2. He had brought me through other physical and emotional challenges, and would again.

But what was my part? I was at a point on my bridge where I could stand still and wait to be rescued, OR, I could start taking very intentional steps forward.

Well, those were the days of television exercise shows. I joined in every morning. Flipping through the channels, I'd go from one instructor to the next celebrity. Pain. So frustrating. I was sick of it!

I began my own research. I loved exploring and finding answers, especially when it came to finding a *better* way to do something. I wasn't a quitter, and I knew God always made a way. Why not here? Why not now? I put my gifts and strengths and belief system to work for me.

I visited medical professionals and asked a ton of questions. With the information they gave me, and my own exploration of my body, I discovered four essential steps for myself, when creating movement:

1. Know the purpose of the movement.

2. Be in my best alignment first.

3. Make every movement intentional at every point.

4. Always maintain or regain my best alignment.

Wow! I tried. I practiced. I tweaked. I shifted. I rested. I kept moving. It all worked! But wait … there's more!

Stability. Stability became a critical piece before and during every movement, and that wasn't something anyone had ever shared with me. It was something I experienced, and it made a BIG difference.

Finally, it was *my* time! I began to see, more and more, the benefits of all my hard work. I was going to feel better! I was going to have a new "normal."

Every morning, I tried what I knew to be true while doing the exercises with the TV shows. Sure, the "experts" said to do "this or that." But it was different for me, because I was *intentional*. I wanted the best for me.

There was so much more to exercise than moving air. (Yeah. Take that one in. It became a purpose for me.)

Here's the best part: after about six months of my consistent mindfulness and effort, I was pain free! The chronic back pain I had lived with since that car accident in high school was gone! I felt solid. I felt strong. I felt safe.

When I told my husband about the results I'd achieved, his first words were, "You need to market that!" And that, my friends, was the other side of the bridge of pain and discomfort for me.

I had arrived at a new bridge. Entrepreneurship.

My new path was the fitness industry.

Entrepreneurship seemed natural. Afterall, both of my parents were entrepreneurs. So were my oldest sister and her husband. But was it *really* my time? Could I teach others that purposeful movement IS possible, and how to move properly? How to prevent injury, and exercise safely and effectively?

Was it time for me to share the path of new principles I had discovered?

- Don't accept pain and lack of movement as your "normal."

- Step up and take responsibility for yourself.

- Use your strengths and talents to get answers.

- Apply what you learn with love, respect, and compassion.
- Be in alignment.
- Be intentional.
- Be purposeful.

I decided it was.

So I embarked on a new path that was really a series of new bridges—some that were simply places of rest. Some were for more research, education, training, and certifications.

I didn't want the "quick fix" certification, or the "just do this or that" training. And, no, I didn't want the "If it hurts, don't do it" answers. I wanted to know the why's, the purpose, the intentions, the building blocks, and the steps that would empower me with what I needed to give to others. So I've stacked my education, training, certifications, and experiences over decades.

After several years of offering employee fitness programs, and working in gym and country club environments, I founded my company, Lab-Fit-Ory, and opened my own office in 1989.

My company is now MasterWellness, working with the whole person, and the path here has been long and sometimes hard. I've struggled with the mindset and perspective of others. I've had children, moved a few more times, started over again, and again. But … I refused to stop moving forward. And when it hurt, I found out why. I got back into alignment. I made sure there was stability. I. Kept. Moving. Maybe not at the pace of others in my industry. Maybe not to the degree of some. But in my time, for my time, I've done well.

And my marriage? At this writing, we just celebrated 40 years!

I'm SO thankful for my faith, my mindset, my life, and … movement.

What about you? Are you happy with how you feel in your life as it is? If not, maybe it's *your* time, now.

My best advice is to refuse to settle for the "If it hurts, don't do it" mindset. Life can be painful! And that pain can lock you up across your life.

So get out there. Take responsibility for your life. Go for your dreams. Research. Get answers. Try. Practice. Tweak. Shift. Rest. Be intentional, for Pete's sake! Make sure you're moving more than just air. Right?

And this is a BIG one: ask for help. A huge part of my getting across every bridge I've faced was asking for help. I prayed. I talked to professionals. I researched. I took steps. I fell down. I got up.

YOUR TIME IS NOW! Whatever bridge you're facing, face it armed with your gifts and strengths. Ask for help. Be intentional in your movement. Take small steps forward (always forward). Rest when you need to, and regain your alignment. Be in touch with where your stability comes from. Use it before and during movement.

And who knows? Maybe, just maybe, getting yourself in better alignment with who you are, recognizing and utilizing your gifts and strengths, asking for help, and taking action will get YOU out of pain and on to purposeful movement across the bridges of YOUR life.

Deni Carruth

facebook.com/yourbridgeisnottoofar

linkedin.com/in/denicarruth

instagram.com/ecoachdeni

Deni Carruth is a fitness expert and nutrition and life coach who helps women create a lifestyle they embodies ease and JOY. She's a lifestyle strategist, working with the whole of who her clients are, for results across their life. When Deni isn't working, she's creating … connections, friendships, graphics, journals, and music. She loves movement, bridges, benches, fresh air, and random rain showers. You can learn more about her here: denicarruth.com.

Get Deni's free gift, **"Your Life From a Glass Half-Full Perspective,"** here now, and learn her step-by-step solution for moving forward and producing a harmoniously exuberant chain reaction across your life, with less effort: hopebookseries.com/ytindeni.

Chapter 15

Your Business's Secret Weapon
(It May Not Be What You Think!)

By Susan Tillery

Jackie Robinson once said, "Our lives are unimportant, except for the influence we have on others."

I've always believed this, which is the reason my first career was in education. I earned a Bachelor of Science in Education with a triple major in Health, Science, and Physical Education, and a Master of Science in Education Curriculum and Instruction. I spent 35 years working in multiple schools and districts, winning Educator of the Year several times. I created and facilitated numerous successful programs, many of which I fully funded with grants I'd written.

Even though, from the outside, everything looked fantastic, on the inside, I was burned out and on the brink of collapse. I suffered from brain fog, fatigue, chronic inflammation, and chronic respiratory infections. Needless to say, I was completely worn down.

I retired early, but other than stepping away from that busy work schedule, my habits didn't change … not my eating habits, not my exercise habits, and not my mental and emotional habits.

Despite the fact that I was no longer working full-time, I still didn't prioritize myself or my health. Then I received a wake-up call.

One fall, I went on my dream trip with my family to the mountains just above Durango, Colorado. During a guided horseback ride, I dislocated my ankle.

Although I was able to finish the ride, I spent the rest of the trip at the lodge, with my parents taking care of me (they were 84 at the time—I should have been taking care of *them*!). Losing some of my independence and being forced to rely on others was not something I felt comfortable with.

If there was a silver lining, it was that this injury forced me to slow down and reflect… not only on how I'd gotten to that point (I played college basketball on a scholarship and spent my career teaching others how to live healthy lives, but I'd neglected my own health), but also on how out of alignment my habits had gotten with how I wanted to live my life. I had destroyed my own health—my most valuable asset. Even in retirement, I wouldn't be able to do the leisurely things I'd planned. I wouldn't even be able to help my aging parents as I'd always imagined I would.

This was my wake-up call. *This* was the moment I realized it was time to focus on my health—and to make some drastic changes.

As soon as I returned home from that family vacation near Durango, I pulled out the six months' worth of health supplements my friend Amy had recommended that I had never taken. It was called Plexus; specifically, a combination of supplements called the Triplex. Looking back, I often wonder why it took such a dramatic event to get me to take action. If only I had known that they key to it all was my own self-care …

Self-care is the secret sauce that gives you the edge, the energy, and the confidence to take action. When you begin to take care of yourself, the results multiply, creating a snowball effect. I had let overwhelm keep me from taking action. But what I came to realize is that overwhelm can be defeated by taking one small step.

Self-care is not one big thing. It is the small hinges that can swing big doors. It's a process that starts from an initial state of small significance and small habits (in my case, simply giving my body the supplements it needed to help with sugar cravings and balancing my blood sugar). Within a short time, the results of those small habits build, creating a significant impact on your life (and your business). I will never get that time back that I wasted in not taking action. But, hopefully, I can encourage and inspire others to take action, now.

Within just three days of starting to take the Triplex, I was amazed at the difference they made in my energy levels. I felt *great*. The more I learned, the more determined I became to make whatever changes were necessary to get me back to the fully healthy, vibrant, and independent person I once was.

My curiosity was piqued: *why* did these supplements work? What was the science behind them?

I started to research Plexus Worldwide, LLC, and learned that it's a leading health and happiness company featuring a full line of health and wellness products that enable people to improve their lives and well-being. It's among the 15 largest direct sales companies in the country, and the top 30 in the world, according to Direct Selling News. Although, when I'd first signed on as an Ambassador (to get the products at a discount), I'd been interested in the income potential my friend Amy mentioned, I never really thought I'd actually work the multi-level marketing business myself.

It just happened naturally.

The curiosity of my friends and family members was piqued, too: they wanted what I had—energy, vitality, health … happiness! They started asking me to get them the supplements, and they, too, experienced incredible results. I soon realized I now owned my own health supplement business—based on products that really worked—and that people were asking for.

Still, even as my friends, family, and I were seeing drastic improvements in our health and happiness, something was missing: we all needed more information about what we should eat, and many of us struggled with things like sugar and coffee addiction. The supplements were a great tool to get us started, but we needed something that would help us make lasting lifestyle changes.

At first, I thought that with my background in science, health, and physical education, I'd be able to map out a plan for myself.

But what I discovered is what's true for so many others: knowing what to do is not enough to make lasting habit changes. I needed support and accountability.

So I began to research the science of habit change.

I found Health Coach Institute, a coaching certification program that seemed promising: more than 10,000 people from more than 30 countries in the past 10 years had completed the program, which promised to pioneer the new generation of health coaches who will change the consciousness of the planet.

There were two things that really interested me most: first, the Health Coach Institute's curriculum. It's based on cutting-edge psychology, brain science, intuitive listening, habit change, and healthy lifestyle design. As I went through the program, I received so much more than my Health and Life Coaching certification … it was truly a life-changing experience. As my physical health improved as a result of what I was learning, I was amazed at how much my mental and emotional health improved, too. It felt so good to be healthy AND happy once again. All I wanted to do was share what I'd learned with others so they, too, could experience the kind of renewed health and vibrancy and happiness I was experiencing!

Second, I knew the negative impacts of being constantly busy, working harder, striving to do more, better, all the time. Our society dictates that this is what we "should" be doing, but I knew firsthand that this lifestyle is detrimental to our health. I loved the idea of becoming an entrepreneur not only because I have gifts to share, but also because I could run my own business online and enjoy the kind of freedom I never could as an educator. It would give me time freedom and the freedom to earn as much as I want, to choose who I work with, when I work, and where I work from!

I knew how valuable these things were for me, and I felt so grateful that since I'd retired, I had the time and space in my life to take a deep dive into what I needed to know to change my habits and get healthy. But I recognize that not everyone has that time and space … I realized there was absolutely nothing more important than helping others be their very best—for themselves, for their families, for their careers and businesses, and for the world!

Finally, I felt like I had all the pieces. My Plexus health supplements were excellent tools. When I combined them with my new understanding of habit change (which I'd gained through my health coaching certification), I knew I had something truly special to share with others … something that would transform lives!

That's why I launched my business, Level Up Health and Wellness. In many ways, being a health coach is so similar to what I've done my entire career as an educator, which is to influence others through education. But what is so unique about health coaching is that a coach's main job is to help his or her clients learn about themselves. It's to help them realize the profound effects of the thoughts they have, the foods they choose to fuel their body, the amount of rest they give themselves, and all the things they do (or don't do) for themselves, on every other aspect of their lives.

There is no way I would have had the energy or confidence to launch and run my own health supplement and health coaching business had my mindset not shifted to embracing the importance of self-care.

My business has since grown to include a full spectrum of programs, including one-on-one health coaching, online group health coaching programs, and my signature Level UP Your Life Vision Board Retreat.

YOU have unique gifts to share with the world, just as I do. You can share them effectively through your business only if you've prepared your body, mind, and soul to be at their peak.

How do you do that? You take your own self-care off the back burner, now. Don't wait, like I did. If I'd started taking those supplements when I first ordered them, I may have had the energy and positivity to begin my business sooner.

Make self-care part of your life every day. Self-care is the absolute best form of healthcare!

Self-care boosts productivity, creativity, and mental health— all of which play a huge role in the success of your business (and in your physical and mental health as your business thrives!).

Here are some questions to ask yourself, to determine whether your habits are setting you up for success in sharing your gifts through your business (answer these questions without self-judgment, but with curiosity):

- **Have you surrounded yourself with positive people** who uplift you and support your pursuit of your goals? Healthy, supportive relationships are a critical part of self-care as you begin taking action to make your dreams reality.

- **Do you regularly celebrate your wins** (the small accomplishments you achieve in the pursuit of your bigger vision)? As goal-oriented people, most of us complete a project or meet a deadline and then immediately move on to the next one. I encourage you to hit the pause button with yourself and your team once a month (or once a quarter) and reflect on what went well or felt satisfying. This kind of reflection can help you and your team stay connected to your passions and purpose.

- I know you're a master of to-do lists. But **do you have a do-not-do list?** If not, would you consider making one that includes sanity-boosting items like not checking email before and after a certain time each day, not using technology on certain days of the week, or not taking work calls during family time?

- **Do you ask for help?** Have you considered hiring someone to help with business items like social media posts, research, or travel planning, or home-related things like house cleaning, yard work, and laundry?

- **Have you taken time to declutter** your office or work-space and home? What can you do to create a sanctuary that brings your energy level up and boosts your mood?

- **Do you take notice when you've slipped out of self-care mode?** In times of stress, self-care can get especially off-balance. Be aware, with self-compassion, of when you've lost touch with your authentic self. Don't waste time being judgmental. Instead, remain curious. Ask yourself what caused you to get off track and what can you do differently next time.

- And last, **how would practicing self-care boost your business** in terms of productivity, creativity, mental health, and/or mood? And how would improvements in those areas boost your business and/or bottom line?

YOUR TIME IS NOW! You already know you have a gift to share with the world. Until now, though, you may not have realized that a HEALTHY YOU is your most important business asset! You ARE worth it.

When you take care of yourself, physically, mentally, and emotionally, you're better able to use your business to change the world.

Susan Tillery

facebook.com/LevelUpWithHealthCoachSusanTillery

Instagram.com/SusanITillery

Susan Tillery, the CEO and Founder of Level Up Health and Wellness, has a Master of Science in Education degree and is a Certified Health and Life Coach. With more than 30 years of experience in teaching biology, health, and fitness education, she has curated a plethora of resources and tools to help you get to your next level on your health journey. You can learn more about her here: leveluphealthandwellness.com.

Download Susan's eBook, **"Self-Care: Your Business's Secret Weapon,"** at no cost, here: hopebookseries.com/ytinsusan.

Chapter 16

No More Waiting for "Someday"

By Ashley Doan

I have *always* been a strong, confident woman who believed she could do ANYTHING she set her mind to, without anyone's help. I never imagined this mindset would eventually contribute to my downfall as a mother and as a woman. Oh, and I'm stubborn, too. *Really* stubborn.

In fact, this combination has worked to my advantage throughout my life. If I set my mind on something I really want, there is no stopping me (especially if it puts me in the limelight)!

I remember studying for a science test in sixth grade—memorizing nine pages of facts about the planets.

I printed out pictures, glued one to each page, colour coded everything, and put it all in a DuoTang. I spent hours walking around our house (because exercise stimulates your brain and memory retention) with my notes in hand, reading them over, and over, and over again (of course, giggling every time I got to "Uranus").

My stubborn dedication to do well on that quiz resulted in a 98% score!

In high school, I signed up for every school talent show, played a leadership role in student council, starred in all the school plays, and strutted my stuff in my school newspaper as Editor.

My stubborn determination continued to serve me. I was intent on having a great career and finding the perfect man, and I did both of those things, as well.

I also knew I wanted to be a mom.

In fact, my first 28 years on the planet convinced me that I was *born* to be a mother! I could feel it in every cell of my body.

I was raised on 80s and 90s television and movies, where quite often, the mother stayed home to raise the children. She always seemed to love every minute of it, with the exception of the minor comical "crisis" in each episode. It looked so easy! So natural.

When I finally had our first child (my son) at 29, I strived to be what I thought was the "perfect" mom: the "good" nurturer who put her life and career on hold to raise her children (even while secretly holding on to the possibility of returning to work "someday," when her kids were old enough to go to school full-time).

But it wasn't as easy as TV moms June Cleaver (Leave It to Beaver), Carol Brady (The Brady Bunch), and Peg Bundy (Married with Children) made me believe.

I had always planned to stay home with our kids while they were young. Even though I loved my career and my work, I thought I'd be okay with leaving the workforce for five to seven years to raise our kids. Yes, I wanted to be my own version of that "perfect" TV mom. But I also thought it was practical. In Vancouver, Canada, where we live, childcare spots are hard to come by. And if you do get a spot, you spend almost an entire salary on daycare! So, not only would I never miss a moment of their early childhood, but it would actually save us money. These were my intentions, anyway, while keeping the thought of returning to work "someday" in the back of my mind.

I knew my time would come again. One day, I'd have my turn in the spotlight again, doing the work I loved! But at that time, I was going to be a mom. And *only* a mom.

Alas, when my son was just an infant, I ended up going back to my 9-5 job for a while to help pay off some of our debts. It was quite a struggle to manage a job and a baby, but we did it.

About 10 months after returning to work, we found out we were expecting our second child. So, I wrapped up my job a few months later, and began re-settling into my role as a stay-at-home mom for the next five years.

In May 2016, ever so graciously at 5:30 in the morning, my daughter made her speedy entrance into this world! Just 12 hours after her arrival, we were driving home … a "perfect Millionaire's Family" (just as I had wanted—two-point-five children: one boy, one tiny, healthy girl with a head full of hair, and our little Jack Russell!).

You know that feeling that washes over you when you board a plane to Hawaii, the Caribbean, or some other exciting vacation spot? That excited anticipation you can feel throughout your entire body, brimming with excitement about what lies ahead?

That's exactly how I felt during that car ride home. I had just had a natural, drug-free birth, and I remember thinking how, if I could handle that, I could handle anything the world might throw at me!

After all, I thought … *I'm an experienced mother! I've been raising our son for two years already. All this newborn stuff will be a breeze!*

Hardly.

Our first week with a newborn and toddler went as expected—the baby nursed and slept. I occupied my eldest with the iPad, and he seemed content. But it didn't take long for the pressure to start building. You see, I had forgotten to take into account that while I was doing all the "easy" newborn stuff, I still had a two-year-old active toddler to keep entertained and alive at the same time!

It didn't take long before handling the "terrible-twos" and a newborn started taking its toll on me. It took every ounce of energy I had to stay awake and make sure our daughter was nursed when she was hungry (she refused bottles, so I was doing all the feedings), and our son was occupied and fed before he got cranky.

I was averaging about three-to-four hours of broken sleep each night. Since the kids rarely synced their daytime naps, I was awake all day, too.

The days melded together, repeating the same monotonous routine: out of bed, shower (sometimes), spend 100% of my already drained energy levels to keep my kids alive until bedtime, then sleep in one- to two-hour increments all night in between children waking up.

Salon days for momma? Nope!

Date nights with hubby? Absolutely not!

Privacy peeing? No way, Jose!

I'm making light of it, yes. But the truth is, I started to give up hope on *ever* having "me" time (or a life … or a career …) again. And I was frustrated. I yelled a lot. I cried a lot. I was not in a good place.

The only thing that helped me survive the days was clinging to the "This too shall pass" adage. It was only temporary, right? It would get better!

Someday, they would sleep. *Someday*, I would sleep! In just five years, they'd be in school. Surely then, I could regain some independence. I could work again. I could poop alone!

Someday!

I clung to that hope like a lifeline.

About eight months into my frustratingly monotonous new life as a zombie-like stay-at-home-mom of two, I was abruptly (as always) woken at 2:00 am by my daughter's cries.

I shuffled into her room and sat in the rocking chair in near darkness, my daughter at my breast. To prevent myself from falling asleep with her in my arms, I began "falling down the Pinterest rabbit hole" on my phone, as one does while nursing a child at 2 am.

While waiting for a (slow) webpage to load, I glanced down at my daughter. Her big, brown, innocent eyes stared back at me with such love, admiration, and hope. Maybe it was my tired state, but something about her eyes that night gave me the kick in the pants I needed to jolt myself out of the zombie funk I'd fallen into.

What was I doing?! My two incredible, beautiful, innocent children looked to me for inspiration for their life. These were the years when kids develop their core belief systems (from birth to seven years of age), which meant that *everything I was doing would imprint on them for their whole lives!* Whatever I did now would be filed in their brains as "normal, expected" behaviours.

What wisdom was I imprinting on these tiny humans when I was grumpy, bored, and neglecting myself while I waited for "someday"?

I didn't want either of them to ever feel the same loneliness and loss of individuality I was experiencing. I wanted them to live a more balanced life—considerate of the needs of others while making themselves a priority, too.

For three years, I had been waiting for "tomorrow." I'd have a life and career again "one day." But what was that waiting telling the little girl in my arms? To wait for her dreams to come true "someday"? To delay taking action to live them now?

NO WAY!

My mindset changed right then and there. While my children had been (and always will be) a huge part of my life, they are not my WHOLE life. My "stubborn determination" to be a perfect "Judy Cleaver" mom was causing me to neglect myself … which was affecting everything and everybody in my family. Not only that, but it was affecting my emotional AND physical well-being. Even though I had lost the baby weight shortly after having our daughter, I then gained 20lbs in her first year! I weighed more than I had when I was nine months pregnant.

The truth is, while I have always been beyond grateful for my family and everything we have, I had focused so much on making our "perfect" life happen, that I forgot to make MY life happen.

I knew it was time for change.

So, in the days and weeks that followed, I became more aware of my actions and emotions. I made more time for myself. And perhaps most importantly of all, I decided that I COULD work and raise my kids at the same time—and I could be great at both.

It gets even better. I decided that, instead of working in a 9-5 as a copywriter and marketing consultant, it was time to start my own copywriting business! I felt a calling to help other working mothers with their business content marketing, so they could spend more time in their business and with their families, while enjoying their passions.

I joined several local business and women networking groups, which was so beneficial on my business-building journey AND for me, personally. It got me out of the house again, enjoying adult conversations (instead of those around kid bowel movements)! I got to use my brain in a completely different way than when I'm at home with my kids, and I loved it. Plus, thanks to the support of the relationships I've made in my networking groups, my business is nearly 100% referral-based today!

And there's more—I'm currently following my calling to help working moms find their own paths, like I did, by getting my holistic life coach certification!

YOUR TIME IS NOW! You too can STOP waiting for "someday," and START prioritizing YOU today! You don't have to trade a career that fulfills you for motherhood. It doesn't have to be one or the other. In fact, whatever your dream is, you don't have to wait even one more day to chase it. Get out there and make it happen!

Ashley Doan

facebook.com/Writergalmarketing

linkedin.com/in/ashleydoan

instagram.com/writergalmktg

Ashley "WriterGal" Doan, international best-selling author and founder of WriterGal Marketing, helps women entrepreneurs use content marketing to reach more people in more ways with their businesses. She focuses on online marketing processes that are easy to execute for even the busiest entrepreneur. She is also an acclaimed public speaker on marketing and working-mother topics. You can learn more about her here: writergal.ca.

Get Ashley's FREE **six-step online course** for busy entrepreneurs who want to learn how to set-up a robust content-marketing program to help grow their business, but spend less time actually doing it, here: hopebookseries.com/ytinashley.

Chapter 17

The Choice Is Yours

By Cyndi Walter

I grew up in a little yellow house on Clearview Avenue. I can't say I have a whole lot of memories from my childhood in that house, but those I do have, I recall with startling clarity.

In one of my earliest, I was about eleven years old. I was woken from sleep by screaming coming from the kitchen, right down the hall from my purple bedroom. I could tell it was my parents, and in my fear, I opened the bedroom door to see what was happening. I could see directly into the kitchen. My dad's glasses were hanging crooked on his face. Blood from an unseen source dripped down to his chin. He was fighting to keep my mother at arm's length as she wildly swung her fists at him. I had no way of understanding the scene before me, and no way of stopping it from happening.

So I ran from that yellow house, in the middle of the night, to a neighbor's where I hoped to fall back asleep.

Throughout the days (and years) that followed, I took care of myself in all the ways my parents couldn't. I babysat for money for clothes. I cooked myself ramen noodles for dinner. And I found relationships that allowed me to feel some semblance of love. But as I learned to take care of myself, I continued to feel a constant pull backward by my existence in that yellow house. I couldn't see all the ways that environment was still affecting me, but I could feel that it didn't want to let me go. Much in the way the smell of my parent's cigarette smoke never quite left my clothes, their behaviors and mindsets went everywhere with me, shading my view of the world with their lenses.

As I started to make my own money … as I found a desire to be educated … as I found the love of my life … I *still* heard the voices of my childhood. "You're insane for thinking you could do that." "You'll never amount to anything that matters." "How dare you think you're better than you are."

But then one day I realized, I wasn't hearing *truth*. I was just hearing the echo of voices from my past. I took a look at my life and realized that, even though I was told I couldn't, I was putting myself through school. Even though I was told I wasn't loveable, there were guardian angels popping up in my life to show me love when I needed it most. And even though I was surrounded by unhappiness, I found joy in working and providing for myself.

Everything I was seeing poked holes in the validity of the voices I had grown up listening to. In that moment of clarity, I had an epiphany: *I get to choose the voices I listen to.*

I had given airtime to the wrong voices for a (really) long time, and they had done nothing but bring me down. They made me feel weighted and limited. They kept me from seeing what my life could actually be.

But in the absence of those voices, the options were suddenly limitless! And even better, my going after them made as much sense as anything else in the world. I woke up to the fact that I could vocalize a desire for a different kind of life, and in doing so, I could make that future a reality.

By the age of 18, I had envisioned the most important part of my future. I made it "real" by describing it under my senior picture in my high school yearbook: "Cyndi Ferrante – Someday, I'm going to have a big, happy family." In making that statement, I put it out into the world that my life *would* be different than the one others envisioned for me. I had no control over the life I was born into, but now, I did have a choice.

I could continue to accept belief systems (instilled in me by my parents) that felt fundamentally wrong, *or I could choose to step into a life of my own making.*

Now, reading that, the choice probably sounds like an easy one, right? Well, not so much, when you consider how terrifying it is to step away from the only way of life you have ever known, no matter how bad that way of life might have been. In other words, this is much easier said than done.

For instance, as I began dating, I found myself in unhealthy relationships that made me feel unworthy, strengthening what I was made to believe growing up with my parents. I had never felt worthy of love, even though I craved it. I wanted a loving relationship, of course. I wanted to *choose* that, for myself. But in actuality, I feared that unknown in comparison to the shallow, albeit hurtful, relationships that I knew so well.

I was also raised in a household that was always lacking financially. We "got by," but my parents held a deep resentment toward the world for not having more. Because we wanted more, we spoke poorly of those who had more—people who flaunted their materialistic possessions. Well, as I began working multiple jobs to put myself through college, I found myself in a familiar state of financial stress. I was going into debt, and I wanted out of it … but lacked even the scantest scaffolding of a foundation of healthy money practices.

I was raised to believe that health is purely external. In order to be healthy, I had to look a certain way. It didn't matter what went into my body, or how my body was used, so long as I looked the part. So, knowing I wasn't worth much, I didn't think my health was worth looking into further, even though I had felt unsettled by my lack of energy and vibrancy.

Even though I had been able to envision a future for myself, these mindsets (and others) held on tight as I tried to shake them off. They would have successfully continued to do so, too, if it weren't for one thing: *I was aware of them.*

I was aware that they hadn't come from me. I was aware of how limiting they were on my life. And I was aware of my very real need to let them go. In this awareness, I found that I didn't have to identify with mindsets forever. Instead, I'm extremely capable of choosing mindsets for myself and shedding those that don't serve me.

Though the process was long and excruciatingly uncomfortable at times, I released each of those limiting mindsets I described above in search of my own that would serve and support me.

I already understood how the journey toward the life of your dreams starts with the ability to envision. I also knew that it continues through action—we have to take action if we want to shift the way we see and understand the world. Luckily, we have seeds of intuition planted within us to lead us along this journey.

For me, the seeds of intuition grew from a passion for fitness, health, and wellness. As early as during my college years, I taught fitness classes, because doing so allowed me to both pay for school and serve other people in a meaningful way. I may not have paid much attention to that passion at the time, but I continued to explore my own fitness: finding running, beginning to road race, and eventually entering the marathon circuit. For years and years, I didn't see how that passion might also serve as a career, but I was experiencing profound personal growth. I was seeing the direct correlation between investing in my health and feeling good. I was learning that I could put certain foods into my body to better fuel my performance. I was feeling better as a human after taking the time to train for races. Most importantly, I was beginning to understand how absolutely and irrevocably worthy I am.

In my 40's, my health was the best it had ever been. I was running my personal best marathon times; I was waking up energized; I was living each day to the fullest. And that's when it hit me … *I was meant to help others achieve the same level of health I had.* And I knew I could help others turn around limiting mindsets to transform their existence, feeling good and living great, just as I had done for myself.

So I started a coaching business, taking on clients who need help balancing their lives in order to feel the way they are meant to. All that was required of me to do so was the passion that had always been inside of me, my personal experience which gave me credibility, and a foundational drive to serve others.

My clients *need* leadership to help them break old and limiting mindsets, so they can step into a healthy and vibrant life.

And when I am selfless in my desire to help them—when my main goal is to see people living more fully—my clients trust me to take them on a very personal and challenging journey to a healthier life.

That trust serves as the foundation of my business, which quickly became a movement. I started making the kind of money that is comically out of line with the financial mindset of my upbringing. And to my shock and amazement, it didn't make me a bad person! It actually made me increasingly humble and charitable. I had already come to see myself as worthy, but now, I was transcending that belief to see that I am *necessary*. In generating income for myself, I am called and able to do more for my community. And from there, I experienced the power of abundance, seeing how as I believed myself worthy of money, more money flocked to me.

With this abundance mindset, I have been able to design a life for the family I dreamed up all those years ago—a family built on a healthy foundation of worth and love. After years of supporting our family as the sole provider, my husband is now able to balance work and life on his terms as I contribute to our income. My four children have attended the colleges of their choice without taking on the student loans I had to work so hard to pay off. They have begun traveling the world, embracing that travel as one of their greatest life teachers. They've moved across the country because they can. They've quit corporate jobs to chase entrepreneurial dreams!

Most importantly, they have inherited positive mindsets that allow them to courageously step into the unknown and grow as people, instead of limiting mindsets that need to be shed like layers of old skin.

We don't all get such a lucky start. The reality is that a lot of us inherit *really* negative mindsets. And even worse, we don't get support in developing better, healthy, empowering mindsets. Rather, we face hate and rejection for thinking another way of life might be better.

While it's hard to face negativity when you're working toward positive change, it's so important to face that resistance with empathy. Any hate and resentment you feel toward those you inherited your mindsets from will only slow down your growth. I encourage you to take a moment to respect the strength of mindsets, positive or negative, and accept that everyone is doing the best they can. Surround the people challenging your mindsets with love and grace, and you will find yourself ready for the next level.

YOUR TIME IS NOW! In every passing moment, you have the opportunity to choose the mindsets shaping your world. If you feel stuck in your career, unhappy in your relationships, or maybe you just feel knots in your stomach that are telling you something is off, look to your mindsets. Ask yourself where your mindsets came from. If you don't like the answer, you can choose to let go and find a mindset that feels right and serves you well.

I promise you, the potential for positive change far outweighs the risk of the unknown. Your passion was placed inside of you for a reason, and there are people relying on you to follow your passion. Furthermore, the growth along the journey is worth every single ounce of discomfort you feel on the way. Your life is built on the mindsets you choose, and the choice is completely yours.

Cyndi Walter

facebook.com/cyndi.walter

instagram.com/cyndiawalter

Cyndi Walter, founder of Cynergy, Inc., embodies a "come as you are" mentality and has attracted a team of over 40,000 people who are working together to release limiting beliefs and habits in order to create the lives they dream of. She is a super-mom, marathon runner, and unstoppable entrepreneur thanks to her mastery of mindset. You can learn more about her here: cyndiwalter.com.

And get Cyndi's free **Healthy Living Guide**, which includes her recipes and tips for starting a new, healthy lifestyle, here: hopebookseries.com/ytincyndi.

Chapter 18
The Qualitarian

By Dez Stephens

I used to live my life thinking more was more—I valued quantity over quality.

And I think that's a common misconception that applies to ALL areas of our life. I'll give you some examples.

Think about your food choices. Whether you're a meat eater, vegetarian, or as my niece says, "cheese-atarian," do you consider the quality (or lack thereof) of the items you choose to consume? You might not be as concerned with quality over quantity if, for example, you notice yourself mindlessly eating an entire bag of Veggie Straws while watching *Netflix*, or eating your kids' stale animal crackers "just because."

How about decision making ... everyday choices? Let's use food again here, since we can all relate. Chocolate—while many of us enjoy it, very few are having a heightened experience with it. I, myself, have become quite the chocolate snob! Those who know me really well buy me Vosges chocolate bars for my birthday. I have become such a "qualitarian" that I can't even stomach a Hershey's bar!

There's also this in-between place we often straddle. Dove chocolate, for instance. It's not the best quality, but it's also not the worst. If I buy a bag of Dove small chocolates, I wind up eating 10 of them in a day instead of a third of a Vosges chocolate bar that takes me to a special place.

The quality, for my personal taste buds, of Vosges is super satisfying. It's like the difference between dopamine and serotonin. Dove gives me a boost of dopamine that doesn't last very long, but the higher-quality chocolate moment I experience with Vosges allows me to ride a wave of serotonin.

So again, the tendency here is to value quantity (Dove) over quality (Vosges). How many decisions like this do you make a day?

Now, some people might consider these examples silly, extravagant, or altogether unimportant. But it illustrates what I've learned about myself over time—that *quality is everything.*

And once you take on this understanding, it seeps into every area of your life. Take your relationships, for example. I swear my first marriage broke up over qualitarian issues! My ex-husband would go to the grocery store with my list consisting of rice, milk, spinach, and blueberries, and would return with the cheapest cracked white rice in a big bargain bag, the most inexpensive milk he could find, some spinach from the clearance bin, and non-organic berries to "save money." This would drive me up the wall, because all I wanted was the Uncle Ben's "nice rice" (as I call it) and berries that didn't smell like pesticides. (My current husband gets me, though—he buys organic berries even when they're not on sale. He's a keeper!)

I joke a little here, but the truth is, life is about enjoying the ride. And you may not be enjoying it as much as you could if you're not focused on quality.

I remember a time when I didn't choose quality over quantity. I was working at a pleasant-enough temp job. They liked my work ethic and offered me a position. I thought to myself, "They're nice enough. This is an easy job. I can work here."

Boy, was that a mistake! I was *so* bored. Every day, one thought consumed me: "What have I done?"

I quickly learned how being challenged plays a big part in my feeling fulfilled. I decided that would be the last time I'd ever settle for less than what I *really* wanted in a job. (This was one of the major steps I took in my journey toward becoming a coach!)

Let's take this a step further, now. Think about your money. How are you spending it? When Oprah made her first "big paycheck," she went out and bought some "thirsty, nice towels." They were thick, super absorbent, and luxurious. And using them made her finally feel like she had "made it." (Side note: I feel exactly the same about higher-thread-count bed sheets … so worth it!)

This is not about affordability. It's about spending your money in a way that is highly impactful for you.

Now, think about how you spend your time—our most valuable (and limited) resource. Are you consciously spending it in a way you would be proud of if your life ended tomorrow? Or are you wasting it?

Recently, I had lunch with my son and his friend, during which the three of us decided to focus on having quality time together. So we each chose to put our phones face down on the table. And thanks to that decision, we had a blast laughing about silly things!

Now, normally, I'd have welcomed the phone use, because the kids would be occupied while I caught up on emails (as a business owner, there are always so many emails!). And I'll be honest: even while I was enjoying their company, I was *thinking* about being on my phone—ugh. But let's be real—having our own little worlds in our pocket has basically become part of our culture.

But as it turned out, my 10-year-old son had a question he wanted to ask me that day. "When was the last time you had sex?" (Incidentally, my answer mortified him, and he was sorry he asked. I laughed so hard when he responded, "Ewww. Where?! Was the dog there?")

The point here is that, if we had all been buried in our phones instead of enjoying quality time together, he never would have asked me. And we wouldn't have laughed together, bonding that way. He now has that memory, but had we just "gone with the norm," he would likely forget that lunch altogether as he grows up.

The truth is, time is all we have. Right? And so many of us waste it. We spend so much of it "doing nothing." Think about the number of hours you spend scrolling through social media or answering unnecessary emails. Can you imagine adding it up for a month to see how much time you could have spent doing something more meaningful?

Finally, let's think about how the concept of quality over quantity may be affecting your professional life, right now.

Maybe you're stuck in a 9-5 because it was easy (like I was). Maybe you sacrifice your quality of life because you don't want to "rock the boat." Maybe you're scared of stepping out in a bigger way, to do something more fulfilling, because it means leaving behind what you already know. *So you stay stuck.*

Maybe you're a small business owner who needs to find great people to hire fast, because you have orders to fill or services to provide based on a boom in your business. You *could* choose to hire average people based on your time constraints, but you will ultimately suffer the consequences of a mediocre staff. (Then, I'd have to coach you on that, too!)

Do you see where I'm going, here?

Becoming a qualitarian can go a long way in improving your life, especially as an entrepreneur/business owner. Imagine how much easier it might be for you to achieve the level of success you desire, when focusing on quality greatly increases your efficiency, presence, and overall satisfaction level.

In fact, I'd go as far as to say that, when making business decisions, the *purposefulness* of choosing quality will never steer you wrong.

Let's say you're choosing a graphic designer to do your logo, or a web designer to create your website. Going for the affordable-and-average logo and website will not make a lasting impression on your potential clients. Great design doesn't have to be expensive, but choosing high-quality talent can make all the difference. And when you choose quality, those you are meant to reach with your gifts will be excited about hiring you based on that quality business card or website home page. But without the quality, they may assume you don't value that feature at all, and then move on to someone else.

As a holistic business coach, this principle has benefitted me in many ways. *I choose* how to spend my time and energy. *I choose* to attend only the meetings that matter. *I choose* to "yes" or "no" in a way that honors me and my time.

And I can't tell you how much that has improved my happiness level.

My mission in both my personal life and professional career is to always go for quality. When I'm in a meeting or playing a board game with my family, I'm conscious of being a quality player. My attention is there. My purpose shines. In my work, when I focus on quality, I feel great about my profession each and every day. That in turn enables me to attract my ideal clients and manifest profitable business relationships.

And this is what I want for YOU!

Wondering how you might begin focusing on quality over quantity in your life? Here are a couple of exercises to get you started making choices and decisions based on quality, so you can better enjoy your daily life.

Exercise 1:

Step 1: Notice what you're noticing. Do you notice yourself hating the end of a 60-minute massage because it feels too short? For me, after trying a 90-minute massage, I can NEVER go back to the shorter one.

Step 2: Observe what you're observing. Do you envy others for what they have or how much they're enjoying life? This is not about the "haves" and the "have nots." The truth is, any budget will allow us to choose quality over quantity. (Even if you're buying Ramen noodles—are you buying the cheapo-cheapo ones or the ones that cost 10 cents more?)

Step 3: Be aware. When it comes to your professional expertise, are you aware of how quality plays a part in how you come across to others? Do you notice when you're at your best?

Exercise 2:

Step 1: Write down every project you're currently working on, professionally or personally.

Step 2: Ask yourself, project by project, if it is adding quality to your life.

Step 3: For the projects that get the "no" answer—release them. Even if it's one that you're doing for someone else, and you're afraid of letting him or her down—let it go. You will notice a huge shift in your life when you do!

The qualitarian way extends into every area of your life: the people in it, the places you go, the experiences you choose. But if you don't pay attention to it, you end up draining yourself by doing things like agreeing to have lunch with someone you actually dread seeing, or going out somewhere when you'd rather stay home, or allowing someone else to choose what you do with your time on any given day.

YOUR TIME IS NOW! Many of us seek some form of enlightenment—a sense of purpose or happiness. We forget that those things are already achievable in our everyday lives. We forget that we don't need to "go big," or hustle to be fulfilled.

When you focus on being a qualitarian, you make everyday choices based on quality: from the quality of the food you eat and prepare, to the thoughts you choose, to the company you keep and the words you speak.

So, take a minute and really think about it … how might you add more quality experiences to your life?

Dez Stephens

facebook.com/radiantcoaches

Dez Stephens is the Founder & CEO of Radiant Coaches Academy, a social enterprise and prominent international coach training school that certifies individuals to create vibrant, professional, private practices as holistic life coaches, wellness coaches, and business coaches. She is a certified life coach, master trainer, and marketing strategist. You can learn more about her here: radiantcoachesacademy.com.

Get Dez's free gift, **The Radiant Coaches Academy Career Pack** here, and discover exactly what you need to know (and do!) to take control of your coaching career from the get-go: hopebookseries.com/ytindez.

Chapter 19

When Giving up Isn't an Option

By Melanie Pigeon

I remember the moment I knew I wanted to be a nurse.

I was sitting in the hospital room next to my mom after she underwent surgery. The nurses buzzed around, helping and caring for their patients. Some of them were absolutely amazing, and some were clearly burnt out and in need of a break.

I wanted to do what they did! I wanted to be that nurse who, no matter how tired, would think of every patient as a family member.

So I went to school, and my journey began.

Nursing school was *tough*. Instead of going out with friends, I spent my early 20's doing clinicals at 6:00 am, organ systems and pharmaceuticals ringing in my head.

After graduating with my nursing degree in December of 2005, I spent the next 10 years as an ICU nurse. My roles included bedside nurse, a preceptor (teaching students and new nurses), member of the code team, and charge nurse in the ICU.

I couldn't be happier with my time there! I love what it feels like to help others—to be there when they aren't well. I love to see a thankful smile looking back at me. Even in the hard moments, when a tearful family member has to say goodbye to a loved one, I would hold their hand, and feel grateful to be able to offer support and comfort. I made lifelong friends in my colleagues, and we have shared heartfelt and heart-wrenching moments together that have truly bonded us as family.

Life was good! I loved my career, my amazing husband, our two sons, and living in the country, where we enjoyed fall evenings outside with a burn pile and smores.

However, in 2009, while pregnant with my youngest son, I found out what it's like to be on the other side of what I do, as the patient. I became very ill over the next few years, and was ultimately diagnosed with Lupus and heart-related complications in 2014.

My cardiologist told me to hang up my ICU hat due to the strain on my body and complications with my Lupus. I had hit rock bottom; I was sick, on disability due to my symptoms (seizures, low blood pressure, sever pain, fatigue, and fluid around my heart to name a few), unable to care for my children, and struggling mentally and emotionally as my husband had to "pick up the slack." I thought my career was over, which meant my dreams were over, too. The "me" I used to be was gone.

But I wasn't ready to give up.

Lupus is a chronic illness, so I knew I had a lot to learn. I began searching for healthy tools to help me combat my illness. I knew that "clean" eating and functional/holistic medicine has been known to help prevent, treat, and in some cases heal autoimmune disease. So, driven by my background as a Critical Care nurse and my natural inclination for fixing things, I began to research. I studied nutrition, stress reduction, and essential oils in relation to healing the body.

Although it was difficult to leave the ICU and begin another chapter of my journey, I moved on in 2015. But what would I do?

I thought about the great respect I have for western medicine, and the many doctors and nurses I had met along my own medical journey. However, I felt a "gap" in the preventative side of medicine. Refusing to give up the work I love, I found a new mission: to bridge that gap.

I searched for employment in the prevention side of the health field, and began working as a wellness nurse.

In that capacity over the past five years, I found myself being constantly approached by people who were struggling just as I was. As a result of an autoimmune disease or unknown health issues, they suffer from debilitating daily fatigue, chronic pain, and heart and other organ-related issues.

And that's when my vision was born.

I envisioned being there for people the way I always loved to as a nurse, but in a new, different way, too. I wanted to work with my clients via phone, internet, and/or in person to come up with personalized care plans based on symptom control and understanding of the disease. I wanted to help individuals get the answers to their own battles, and provide them with the tools they need to finally feel better, in a much shorter span of time than what I endured! Perhaps most of all, I wanted to give people a place to turn when their symptoms arose.

And why *couldn't* I? I had the medical knowledge and the experience to help others plan a path to the healthiest version of themselves. I had the natural solutions and nutritional plan that made all the difference in my own health, allowing me weeks without fatigue and fluid around my heart. I knew how to help others keep their inflammation and pain under control.

That's what I wanted to do.

I had created new dreams for myself, and it was time to pursue them.

In 2017, I became a Doterra Wellness Advocate of essential oils, having seen firsthand how beneficial they can be. I also now get the privilege of guiding others with mental health problems, children struggling with focus, and more. I also once again have the honor of working with individuals who are as dedicated to helping others as I am, which is another blessing. We are a team of women (many of whom are also RN friends) who have adopted a full-body wellness approach to health. We empower patients all over the world with the healing properties of care plans, supplements, and essential oils right in their homes!

The message I want to share is this:

It's *not* too late for a new dream!

I worked hard to become a nurse, and still feel honored to be one. I am also proud to have leveraged my struggles into tools that helped me grow as a person. Sure, I could have just given up when I was diagnosed with Lupus … thrown my hands up and stayed on disability.

But that was not an option, for me.

I started over when everything was stacked against me, and I forged a new career path that would still allow me to support people in the way I so loved to.

And I witnessed lives changing! My patients, family, friends, and individuals I met from all over the world have experienced the same transformation I have.

No matter where you are now, you *can* be successful doing what you love. (And remember, if you do have a chronic illness, like me, *it becomes a part of you; it does not have to define you!*)

If you're ready to take control of your destiny, here are a few tips to get you started!

Step 1. Work on your mindset.

Every single day when you wake up, find gratitude. It helps set the tone for a positive day, and supports you in accomplishing the things you put your mind to.

Step 2. Ask yourself if you're happy.

If you're not, what does the picture of YOUR happy life look like? Describe it. Write it all down.

Step 3. Write down your goals.

It's a well-known fact that actually putting them on paper increases your chances of achieving them.

Step 4. Brainstorm how you might be able to support others with your passion.

Make a list of career paths and ideas that would allow you to help people who are undergoing a similar journey as yours.

Step 5. Find support.

Look for groups you can join whose members have the same (or similar) passion as you, so you have likeminded company to motivate you and keep you on track. Find a mentor or coach who can help keep you accountable while you make progress toward your dream!

YOUR TIME IS NOW! Even if you are brand new to the idea of entrepreneurship … even if you are depressed, sick, sick of being depressed, and/or feel a loss of hope, you CAN take control of your own health, livelihood, and destiny! It won't always be easy or the path of least resistance, but you can *make the choice to change your path*, just like I did.

Make it happen! Dig deep and find that new path. It's waiting for you!

Melanie Pigeon

facebook.com/MelaniewellnessRN

instagram.com/melaniewellnessrn

Melanie Pigeon is a nurse and educator, supporting individuals who want to take back control of their health: those who have chronic symptoms and want to discover the cause and solution, and those who have been diagnosed with an autoimmune disease or chronic illness. She is passionate about helping heal those who are suffering, in turn creating happier, healthier families. Learn more about her here: melaniewellnessrn.org.

And get Melanie's free gift, a FREE one-on-one Doterra Essential Oils consult and personalized nurse care plan, by scheduling it here, right now: hopebookseries.com/ytinmelanie.

Chapter 20

Following Your Heart's Path

By Michele PW

There are some people who decide to follow their heart, and everything falls into place beautifully.

I am not one of those people.

I share this because you too might be someone who decides to follow your heart, only to find that it takes a little while for things to click (and maybe, things even get worse before they get better).

I want you to know that it doesn't mean you're not on the right path. It just means that the path is a bit bumpier than what you originally thought. But I get ahead of myself.

My story starts when I was three years old and taught myself to read because I wanted to write fiction so badly.

I wrote my first novel at sixteen, and won a national fiction award in high school. However, along with working on my fiction, I also looked for other ways I could make a living to support myself.

Everyone told me to become a journalist. That was the last thing I wanted to be, so I kept searching. And then, in college, I stumbled onto the world of copywriting.

Copywriting is writing promotional materials for businesses. It has nothing to do with protecting intellectual property or putting a copyright on something like a song or a piece of art (note the difference in spelling).

You see, there's a lot of writing required in a business. But most of it isn't regular work, which is why a lot of writing is outsourced to freelancers rather than hiring writers as employees. Hence, the entire freelance copywriting industry.

I stumbled upon this industry pretty much by accident while still in college. Actually, it would be more appropriate to say freelance copywriting found me—freelance jobs started landing in my lap.

"This is great," I thought, and immediately decided to find a job doing that kind of work, so it would become a steady source of income.

The Universe, however, knew my path lay in another direction. So, while finding freelance writing gigs was easy, finding an actual job was not.

But I was determined, so I kept pushing it. And eventually I got my wish—I ended up landing a couple of agency jobs, a corporate job, *and* a city government job.

But something didn't feel right. I was restless. It wasn't so bad during my first couple of jobs when I was still in Madison, Wisconsin, but I started getting VERY restless after I moved to Prescott, Arizona and got a position in the communications department of the City of Prescott.

This was 1998. I was pretty unhappy there, but didn't feel like I could quit. My husband was in the middle of transitioning out of his first business, and I didn't think we could afford the lack of a steady paycheck.

On the other hand, I was becoming increasingly unhappy. Worse, my relationship with my boss had been deteriorating over the course of six months, and I wondered if I would even be *able* to keep my job.

I took a couple weeks off to visit my family back in Wisconsin. My husband and I had decided I would quit when I returned, and I would start freelancing again.

But then I got cold feet. My first day back, I was all set to turn in my notice when I thought to myself, "Oh, this isn't so bad. And isn't having a steady paycheck better than the uncertainty of freelance work?"

I called my husband to tell him I had changed my mind, and he actually got a little angry with me. He said, "I thought we decided you were going to quit. You're not happy, so quit."

I thought about it and realized he was right. So, I headed over to my boss's office and turned in my notice.

It turned out to be the very best thing I could have done.

I started my freelance copywriting business in 1998, and built it up fairly quickly.

At first, everything seemed fine. But the longer I was in business, the more something seemed "off," and the more I felt that restlessness again.

What on earth was the problem? I was a freelance copywriter—I had the exact same business as other freelance copywriters. So what was going on? *Why* was I restless again?

The answer was actually quite simple: I realized I was an *entrepreneur*, not just a freelance writer. And it became clear to me that I was being called to build an actual company, as opposed to simply creating a j-o-b for myself.

So how did I go from solopreneur to CEO of a multiple six-figure company? I'm sharing five key steps I took, so you can do the same if you're feeling called to it:

1. I took Einstein's quote to heart: "The definition of insanity is doing the same thing over and over and expecting different results."

In December 2004, I made a horrible discovery. For some reason (I'm still not sure why), I decided to go through my Quickbook statements to compare my income from each year. To my disgust, I discovered that I basically made the same amount of money every year ($40,000 to $50,000).

You see, over the years when I was in the "feast" cycle of my business, I would proudly tell people I was "growing" my business. Never mind the "famine" cycles were completely wiping out any gains from the "feast" cycle. I had also raised my rates over the years, yet nothing changed. In fact, my best year was one of the years when my hourly rate was the lowest.

All of a sudden, the realization hit me. I wasn't *growing* a business. I had reached a plateau, and I was stuck there.

Around that same time, I saw the "Seinfeld" episode in which George decides he doesn't like his life (being broke, jobless, living at home, no girlfriend). So, he decides to do everything exactly opposite of how he usually would. And it worked! By the end of the show, he had a girlfriend and a job with the New York Yankees.

So 2005 became the year that I decided to "do the opposite," too, which leads me to number two.

2. I hired a business coach. Once I discovered that I was stuck, I realized that I probably needed some help getting unstuck.

You see, there are two issues you have to face when you become stuck. The first is that you have to realize that *you* are the reason you're in the situation in the first place. And the second is that you actually have to do something to change it.

And it's not as easy as it sounds. Your perspective on yourself, your thoughts, your actions, etc. are cloudy at best. Now there's no question you can create change on your own, but it's a lot more difficult without someone else pointing things out and guiding you.

Plus, there are other benefits to hiring a coach or mentor for yourself. When you do, you tell yourself (and the Universe) that you're ready to take yourself seriously and do what it takes to be successful. You're also saying you're worth the investment. (Because that IS what you're doing—you're investing in yourself by getting coaching, mentoring, and education from someone who has been there already, so you can get to where you want to go a lot faster and with fewer detours.)

Now you do need to make sure you hire the *right* coach or mentor—not all are created equal, so take a little time to make your choice. Don't just pick the first one you come across. Do some research, and ask around to make sure you choose one who is really right for you.

3. I got in alignment with what I teach. In my case, it meant making marketing my own business as important as marketing my clients' businesses. In your case, it may look different. But the reality is, you personally need to be in alignment with what you teach. If you're not, how can you possibly stand tall and value your gifts and brilliance?

Now, I have an important note about this—do NOT use this as an excuse to not move forward in your business. If you feel like you're not in alignment, then get yourself in alignment. The only way you're going to transform your business is if you do what you need to do to be an alignment it, practicing what you preach. (And if you can't get yourself in alignment, maybe you need to take a good hard look at what you're providing. You might need to tweak your offering. This could be a message from the Universe that you're not doing what you're truly meant to do.)

4. I did what I needed to do to work through my blocks. You may have heard the quote (and I'm paraphrasing here) that the best self-development tool is having a business. ALL your obstacles and blocks will show up as you start and grow a business. And don't be surprised if some of the biggest blocks show up when everything looks good on the surface.

I have two suggestions: First, know it is totally normal, and be prepared for it. Second, don't stop investing in yourself. Whatever you need to do to keep moving forward and busting through your blocks, do it. Maybe you need a coach, a product, or something else. Or maybe you need to finally outsource something you've been reluctant to let go of (your copywriting, for instance?).

Chances are you know what you need to do to keep moving forward, so what I want to encourage you to do is to honor that feeling, and start taking action.

5. I took action. Nothing happens if you don't do anything. The best advice I can give you (other than marketing yourself regularly) is to keep taking action. Get those to-do's crossed off your list, and watch your business grow!

Remember, the road CAN be bumpy. Just because you make a decision and start down a specific road DOESN'T mean all your problems magically float away, and you can expect smooth sailing.

Here's an example of what I mean: When I first made the decision to play bigger and grow my business, the exact opposite happened. My business died. For six months.

How did I get myself out of it?

By recommitting to my vison and taking the action I needed to take.

I refused to anything get in the way of my moving forward.

YOUR TIME IS NOW! Just because things get tough after deciding to follow your heart does NOT mean you're not on the right path. You just might need to do something a little differently, or make a deeper commitment.

There's one thing I can promise you:

If you do give up, you're *never* going to see your dream come true. So whatever you do, don't give up.

Michele PW

Michele PW (Pariza Wacek) is a best-selling, award-winning fiction and nonfiction author. On the fiction side, she writes psychological thrillers/mystery/suspense books and has a popular book blog. On the nonfiction side, she's written five books in the "Love-Based Business" series that share how to sell more with love and build a solid, profitable business on a foundation of love. In addition, she owns a copywriting and marketing company that has sold $50M worth of products and services over the past eight years. You can learn more about her at MichelePW.com.

If one of your dreams is to grow a business, get Michele's free gift—a copy of her **"How to Start a Business You Love AND That Loves You Back"** book—here: hopebookseries.com/ytin-mpw. It's full of exercises and questions to help you get clarity on the steps you need to take to grow the perfect business for you. (And yes, even if you have a business, Michele's book can help … especially if it's one you don't love!)

Chapter 21

The Journey—It's Not How You Start That Matters; It's How You Finish

By Rania Loughnan

As a highly driven entrepreneur, I worked tirelessly for years to build a successful business in hospitality. And I loved it! Life was amazing, and I enjoyed every bit of my hard-won success. I was flying high. I was unstoppable—invincible. What could possibly go wrong?

As it turns out, a lot! Let me go back to the beginning.

My journey to entrepreneurial success began out of sheer financial necessity. I had emerged from a problematic and acrimonious breakup homeless, mentally and emotionally battered and bruised, with two small children.

It all began when I spent a season snowboarding in Andorra, Europe. I met and became good friends with a guy, and later, upon returning to England, we started dating. Then, as the saying goes, he "swept me off my feet" with his charm and adoration, and we began living together. At the time, I worked as a Clinical Coordinator in a busy London hospital, and he worked in the construction industry. We shared many interests, so he was definitely my kind of guy.

We got along really well, and he eventually persuaded me to make a life together in his homeland, New Zealand—11, 500 miles (18.500 km) away! He filled my head with stories of his snowboarding days in NZ and painted a picture of the idyllic life we would share. At 24 years old, I'd always been independent and adventurous, so I was not at all daunted by the move. He promised my family and friends that he would take good care of me. Then, trusting him completely, I said my goodbyes and off we went.

Our life together began well. New Zealand was indeed all he had described—breathtakingly beautiful with snow-covered mountains and ice-blue lakes. The people were genuinely lovely and easy-going, too. I secured a job at a medical facility on the ski slopes while he started a construction company. The future was bright, and I'd made the right decision to move there with him—or so I thought!

Within months, the cracks started to appear; my guy was beginning to show signs of a controlling personality. The abuse started slowly at first. He didn't like the way I did this or that, or the way I dressed. He was *always* complaining. I made the usual excuses for him; he was tired, or had a stressful day. I found myself continually appeasing him to make him happy, but it didn't work.

Around this time, I discovered I was pregnant with our first child. My guy appeared to be happy about it, but oddly enough, the mental and emotional abuse continued. I continued to work on the slopes right up until my eighth month, and with no transport of my own, would often have to walk the 40-minute journey home in the snow. He showed no sign of compassion at all. I would naturally be tired, but that just made him worse, and of course, it was all my fault he was unhappy. My happy-go-lucky personality was gradually being eroded, and I would often cry myself to sleep. I sometimes confronted him about his lack of caring, telling him I would leave if he didn't shape up. He would beg me not to go and promise to stop being mean, but each promise was short-lived.

Our first son was born, and like most new parents, we struggled to find our rhythm but muddled through. Seventeen months later, at the age of 28, our second son was born. The abuse continued, but I felt I had to make it work—after all, we were a family.

Though I had two tiny children, I decided to pursue my interest in business management and took two courses, back to back. I graduated with honors. My achievements uplifted me, but my partner showed no interest. He was continually complaining we had no money (even though we did) and pressured me to find work. I was still breastfeeding, so it wasn't easy to find decent daytime employment.

He kept pressuring me until eventually, just to appease him, I took a cleaning job at a nursery school just meters from where we lived. This enabled him to look after the babies when he came home, so I could go to work. So, there I was with two children in diapers, breastfeeding, enduring sleepless nights, running his business, and working a cleaning job … but he still complained I was "lazy."

By the time my boys were two and three years old, my mind was in a dark place, and my self-esteem was pretty non-existent. I had lost so much weight, I was a mere wisp of my former self. The boys were witnessing their father's mental and emotional abuse and were caught up in our constant arguments, which wasn't healthy.

I realized I had to leave my partner for the sake of my children and my sanity. So, finally, six years after moving to New Zealand, I found my opportunity to make a break for freedom.

We had been staying with his mother, and I happened to be there alone with the boys for a couple of hours. This was it! I had a small window of time to jump into action, and instinctively felt it was "now or never." With my heart beating so fast and my legs like jelly, I thought I might faint from fear. I rang a car hire company and quickly packed a few things for the children. I was terrified the family would return as I anxiously waited for the car to arrive. Luckily, they didn't, and I bundled the boys into the hired car and fled to a women's refuge.

Though I was a nervous wreck and had *nothing*, we were safe.

Lost and alone in a foreign land on the other side of the world from my family, I couldn't leave the country because of the children—it was their homeland, after all. So, thank goodness for the support I received at the refuge, as the staff helped with *everything*. They provided food, diapers, clothes, and vital necessities for the babies. Eventually, I was able to receive benefits as a single parent, and the support workers helped me find rented accommodation.

While in the refuge, my ex stripped us of everything except the clothes on our backs and a few dollars in my purse. He emptied the bank accounts and took all our possessions. When I eventually found a place to live, he refused to give me anything we once owned together, including the children's toys. He was hell-bent on making the boys and me destitute to force me back to him. As for financial support, he lied to the authorities and pleaded poverty, even though he had many "boy-toys," including a speedboat, ski-do, and many other expensive items. He was only required to give me less than fourteen NZ dollars a week between the boys! It was devastating.

With my beautiful boys beside me, I had to rebuild our lives from scratch. They needed me to be strong, and I was determined to make a good life for them. So, I did a lot of thinking and planning—what was I good at? As a social butterfly, I'd always felt comfortable with others on any level; rich or poor, they were all people with a backstory.

So, having been a Clinical Coordinator, I combined my social skills with my coordinator skills, added the knowledge from my business courses, and started a company as a wedding and events planner. I didn't need any capital to begin with, which was helpful. Fortunately, I had several high-profile friends and began networking to create a portfolio.

Over the next few years, my portfolio grew, as I organized (among other events) high-profile weddings for the rich and famous. I loved my work and being able to provide for my children. My boys were in preschool by then, which allowed me to concentrate on being a successful businesswoman. We were a happy little family—I'd made it on my own, despite the obstacles.

Then, without warning, I became seriously ill and was twice hospitalized with a mental health breakdown. Everything stopped in its tracks, and I was forced to walk away from the thriving business I'd created. All my hard work was wiped out in that instant. I could no longer meet deadlines or my clients' needs—my life was in chaos in more ways than one. I hadn't realized the impact the abuse and breakup had had on me and my well-being. I had been so busy holding it all together for my children that I'd failed to address the trauma I'd experienced. It was a harrowing time for my children and me.

Completely incapacitated by my illness, I had to mourn the loss of everything I'd worked so hard to build. No one else had a clue how my business operated. Although I employed staff, I was the driving force juggling all the balls, so, the moment I couldn't function, everything fell apart. I was back to square one. What was I to do? How could I calm the chaos?

During my long illness and slow recovery, I had plenty of time to think. I needed to create a fool-proof, reliable system and structure to ensure a secure future, both personally and in business. It would need to be an easy-to-operate system that would enable others to run my company in my absence should I ever become ill again. I quickly learned that, to achieve my goal, I would need to learn to navigate the complexities of 21st-century technology. So, I took a step back and spent the next four years researching IT. Then, using my new-found, tech-savvy knowledge, I developed a system and structure to ensure my business would function smoothly, successfully, and with minimum effort.

The path of discovery into the world of IT was enlightening as I learned about the four main components necessary to achieve my goal. I would have to, Systemize, Automate, Streamline, and Integrate (SASi) every aspect of a company, by using 21st-century technology. I also learned that online marketing and sales are now the primary way of selling any product or service. So I knew I needed to capitalize on technology if my company was to be noticed and competitive, or I'd risk being left behind in this fast-paced, tech-savvy world of commerce. With all this in mind, and through research and trial and error, my new company, SASinnovators™, was born.

Finally, I was back in the saddle: happy, well, and flourishing. I had come such a long way from being a wedding and events planner that technology was now in my blood, and my passion for it unleashed.

Now, I run a successful online company empowering women entrepreneurs to build and maintain a successful business.

I promise you, you CAN emerge triumphant over any obstacles you face.

My advice?

- Stay true to yourself.
- Maintain your integrity.
- Never give up.
- Seek good advice.
- Turn every obstacle into a steppingstone.
- Be willing to learn and change direction.
- Embrace your mistakes.
- Leave the past where it belongs.
- Believe in yourself.

YOUR TIME IS NOW! You CAN accomplish your dreams. If you are inspired to create and build a business, then do whatever it takes to manifest your vision, and LIVE it!

Rania Loughnan

facebook.com/sasinnovators

linkedin.com/in/sasinnovators/

instagram.com/empowering_businesswomen

Rania Loughnan is Co-Founder of SASinnovators™. She is now happily married to her love and rock, James, and together have five boisterous boys. Rania also sits on two government Mental Health and Addiction panels and is actively involved in networking Peer Support Groups. Full of fun, she is also the manager of a local youth rugby team! You can learn more about her here: empoweringbusinesswomen.com.

And be sure to grab Rania's free gift, **From Start-Up to Marketplace**—a comprehensive eBook designed to help woman entrepreneurs and start-ups achieve their vision, here: hopebookseries.com/ytinrania.

Chapter 22

The Light of Change

By Teagan Hintze

There are times in every person's life when everything shifts. Often, this shift occurs during our absolute darkest moments: a door, window, or gate opens, revealing a sliver of light carrying the promise of change. Stepping into that light can be incredibly hard, but it is also an awesome opportunity to grab it up into a massive hug, and to let it guide you into your best life.

My big turning-point moment happened in 2015. After struggling with infertility for 10 years, I was finally a new mom! My son was five months old, and my then husband was a full-time student at the local University. I had been working for a business education company as a Marketing Director for two years, giving it everything I had. I worked 14+ hour days, and took only 10 days off after having my son. I was invested in my work, and in making the company great—to increase its profits and explode its success. And that's exactly what I did.

When I first started, it was just me and one other employee. Since we were small, we were doing two events a month in four states. I grew the team to 35 employees, doing seven events a week in 49 states. I increased the company's revenue 700%. We began doing summits multiple times a month. We built a massive new building. We purchased a seven-million-dollar cabin in Park City to host retreats. We had to bring on additional upper-level staff to handle our clientele load.

In other words, I poured my heart and soul into the company, and it worked.

When I experienced my turning point, we were in the beginning planning stages of hosting a MASSIVE event featuring Gary Vee as our main speaker. I was behind the *whole* thing: I had built a website, locked and secured a venue at the local university, and obtained massive funding. I had even gotten the local business school to go in on it with us. It was going to be incredible—a big step for the company.

One day (like any other, or so I thought), I was called into the owner's office. This wasn't unusual, as I often had meetings with her to discuss new moves, strategies, and ideas for continued growth. We sat down and started our usual chat. How are the kids, what is new, how was your last trip, etc.? But then things changed. Her tone and posture shifted, and I knew something was up. My stomach dropped, my nerves went straight to high alert, and my hands went sweaty as my whole world began to spin. Although I didn't know what was going to happen, I definitely had a feeling of trepidation.

As I sat there across the desk from her, she proceeded to tell me that she was grateful for the work I did. She said I was very skilled and talented at my job, and that I was very hard working. Then came the bomb.

BUT, YOU ARE NOT A LEADER.

I was dumbfounded. At first, I didn't know how to react. I just sat there in silence as she proceeded to tell me that she was demoting me. I was no longer going to be the director; in fact, I was no longer going to be a part of that team at all. I would now be responsible for simply creating graphics and marketing materials. I no longer a part of creative decision making. I was relegated to the corner in a department on my own, without coworkers, a boss, or any motivation. I was removed from the Gary Vee event, taken off all the revenue-producing summits, and kicked out of all upper-leadership meetings.

From that moment on, it was like listening to the teacher on the Peanuts. A blur of "wah-wah-wahs." Nothing audible. Nothing that made any sense. I simply couldn't process.

I walked out of that meeting deflated. I gathered my things and left, going straight to my baby's daycare. I picked him up for some serious snuggles, and we went home.

Since I no longer had to actually go in to work to complete my tasks, the next three days were a blur of working from home, binging on sugary treats and Dr. Pepper, and watching Netflix. But my three-day sulking period ended when I suddenly shifted my perspective—when I saw the sliver of light of promise I mentioned earlier.

I saw the demotion as a window. A giant door, instead of a roadblock.

I perceived it as the universe telling me that if I was going to take a leap, *this* was the time to do it.

So, I decided to go for it ... to create and build my own social media management business! I started with a business plan. I mapped out exactly how I would do it. I created a plan for walking away from the horrid j-o-b that didn't care about me or my goals. I took the time to officially set those goals, and created a home office setup (ok, it was just a card table and a kitchen chair, but it did the job!). I worked my 9-5 while taking care of my little guy. I would make dinner for my little family, and when they went to bed, I would work on my business. I would work until my eyes felt like they were going to melt or fall out of my head, I was so so tired. I would crawl into bed at 2-3:00 am and get a few hours of sleep before my little guy woke up. Then I would do it all over again.

I was determined to not take the door the universe provided me for granted. I was *going* to make it work.

And my hard work paid off. My business replaced my income from my 9-5 in just two weeks! Two weeks of (very) late nights building a website, writing social media posts, working for free for family and friends to validate my idea, and working toward my goal. Two weeks, and I had the same paycheck working for myself as I did from a 9-5 job. So, I went back to the business education company I had worked so hard for, and told them I was finished.

I was *so* relieved ... I was free!

And that changed everything.

I have learned so much during this process of leaving a j-o-b and working for myself. I learned that a person is essentially dispensable, when working for someone else. Usually, the owner of the company doesn't actually care about his or her employee's goals and dreams. They care about their own.

I learned that standing in the shadows doesn't benefit me—that if I wanted a better life for myself and my family, I had to stand up and create the change I sought.

But what does that mean for you?

Well, if your story is similar to mine—if you're working a 9-5 j-o-b, for someone else, stuck on a hamster wheel while you work on someone else's dream … if you're living in terror every time you get called into the office because you're afraid of losing your job … if your nerves are always on high alert, as you live paycheck to paycheck … if you have goals, but no idea how you are ever going to achieve them … know this—the first step is the hardest.

I know, because I have been there, and I was terrified! But here's the thing: once you take it, the next one gets easier. And so does the next one and the next one. Before you know it, you are 5,000 steps in and well on your way.

So how do you start?

First, be authentically you. People can spot a fake 100 miles away (trust me on this one). Especially when it comes to connecting in the online space, which is a bit more difficult to do than it is in person, you've got to get comfortable being vulnerable … and putting yourself out there.

Embrace your story—it is so powerful! Use it to help inspire (and connect with) others. Before you know it, you'll build a network, light your soul on fire, and bring nothing but amazing things toward you!

Next, find something that you either want to learn badly enough to stick with and be one step ahead of your audience, or something you can talk and learn about for DAYS. *That* is what you build your business around.

Then, it's time to create a goal. Make it big—one you have to work for—like replacing your full-time income, or paying off student loans, or taking that insane three-week trip you've been dreaming about. You want to STRETCH to meet it.

From there, you break your goal down into milestones, and in between the milestones, into steppingstones that will get you from that first step to that first milestone. For me, those steps were things like posting on IG every single day, starting an email newsletter, building a website that I was proud of, creating connections, looking for new ways to build, and learning.

Once you have those kinds of steps and systems in place, **_then_ you add in those new exciting projects, courses, and additional clients,** so you scale to the next level. Will it all happen overnight? Nope, probably not. But just keep going!

I want you to know that **YOUR TIME IS NOW!** You can _choose_ to change your situation. Your goals can be achieved. You can dream as big as you want, and you can realize them. They can come true!

You can step into the spotlight and share your gift with others. You can use that gift, that talent, and those skills and gain a better life for yourself. You can make money with it. You can build a business and hire people to help YOU build your dreams!

You get to make that choice. You can take the chance when you see that door, crack, window, or gate … and you can change your life.

Teagan Hintze

instagram.com/msteagancharlotte

Teagan Hintze is a newly married wife and mama to one Mario-obsessed four-year-old. There is a lot in life that she hasn't done and for sure doesn't know, but there are a few things she does know. One: Sweatpants are pants, and no one can tell her otherwise. Yes, she wears them EVERYDAY. Two: Dr Pepper is the best drink ever and she will drink it every day. Yes, they do sponsor her, and yes, she did create a label for them. Three: Sugar is a food group and is totally acceptable as a meal. Four: Sarcasm is quite literally the best thing ever (especially coupled with sass). Five: Reading is a hard-core addiction, because learning is the best. Six: Dance parties will solve any bad mood. She is the founder and owner of She Knows Social, and lives in California with the two men of her life. You can learn more about her here: sheknowssocial.com.

Get Teagan's free gift, the **"Get to Know Me Fill-in-the-Blanks Generator"** (mad-lib style) designed to help you introduce yourself time and time again to your audience, so you sound authentic, creative, and clever as people get to know you, here: hopebookseries.com/ytinteagan.

The AWE Network

The Amazing Women Entrepreneurs Network is a rapidly growing supportive community of tens of thousands of women who are inspired to take their business and life to the next level.

Here, you'll find all in one place the community, accountability, education, support, exposure, opportunities, resources, and inspiration you need to build a thriving business around your unique gifts!

Visit amazingwomenentrepreneurs.com and discover:

• **Several gifts designed to give you expert advice on building your business**, including tips and strategies for increasing your visibility, creating a profitable, automated sales funnel, working toward financial freedom, slaying Instagram, and so much more (new gifts added often)!

• **A content-rich blog, with posts about every aspect of living your entrepreneurial dream life,** such as how to attract more clients with content you already have, what to look for in a coaching certification, how to develop new blog topics, and more.

• **Online training courses designed to help you grow your business,** using proven, step-by-step processes that will boost your income, help you transition from a 9-to-5 to your entrepreneur dream life, and more.

• **Opportunities to increase your exposure** through our vast network of supportive, positive women entrepreneurs.

• And more.

If you'd like a taste of what the Amazing Women Entrepreneurs Network can do for you, check out all the invaluable gifts at amazingwomenentrepreneurs.com/free-goodies.

The Hope Book Series

We're on a mission to create a movement of holistic success for women around the world, by sharing real-life stories of people who were able to create lives they love AND businesses that give them the freedom lifestyle they deserve.

That's what the "Hope Book Series" is all about.

It covers topics including business, money, health, spirituality, careers, life, mindset, overcoming trauma, and transformation.

Published books available on Amazon, and more coming soon!

Become a Co-Author of the Hope Book Series

Being an author or coauthor is GREAT in itself, but there is so much more to it than that. It's about making an impact, creating a movement, and delivering huge value based on experience and results.

If you want to bring your brand or movement into the world in a BIG Way, then the Hope Book Series is for you!

The Hope Book Series is for anyone looking to bring their products, brand, or service into the world with integrity and power that lights up your life. It's about growing a business you are deeply in love with, making an incredible living *and* impact as you help millions around the globe.

Getting yourself or your brand "omnipresent" is the answer to consistency and profits. Because when it comes to success, it's NOT who you know—it's WHO KNOWS YOU!

We too are on a mission to create a movement of success for women around the world, so they can live a life they love and have a business that provides them the freedom lifestyle they deserve.

The Amazing Women Entrepreneurs Network believes it takes five pillars to THRIVE. Those pillars are Business, Wealth, Mind, Body, and Spirit. When one pillar is broken, it affects the others.

We aim to educate and empower women about taking a holistic approach to enjoying a thriving life.

If you love the "Chicken Soup for the Soul" inspirational books, then you will love our Hope Book Series for women.

Right now, we are accepting co-author applications for upcoming anthologies in the "Hope Book Series." To learn more about becoming a contributor, visit amazingwomenmedia.com.

Hashtag It

Join us in our mission to help women across the globe achieve financial independence and live the life of their dreams by spreading the word!

Every month, I'll randomly choose one person to receive a free gift! If you'd like a chance to win, share a photo of you with this book on social media with the hashtag #HOPEBOOKS.